YOUR
HOROSCOPE
2016

♍

VIRGO

YOUR PERSONAL
HOROSCOPE
2016

VIRGO
24th August–23rd September

igloobooks

Published in 2015
by Igloo Books Ltd
Cottage Farm
Sywell
NN6 0BJ
www.igloobooks.com

Produced for Igloo Books by Foulsham Publishing Ltd, The Old Barrel Store,
Drayman's Lane, Marlow, Bucks SL7 2FF, England

Cover images: Thinkstock / Getty

HUN001 0715
2 4 6 8 10 9 7 5 3 1
ISBN 978-1-78440-591-5

This is an abridged version of material originally published
in Old Moore's Horoscope and Astral Diary.

Printed and manufactured in China

CONTENTS

INTRODUCTION

Your Personal Horoscopes have been specifically created to allow you to get the most from astrological patterns and the way they have a bearing on not only your zodiac sign, but nuances within it. Using the diary section of the book, you can read about the influences and possibilities of each and every day of the year. It will be possible for you to see when you are likely to be cheerful and happy or those times when your nature is in retreat and you will be more circumspect. The diary will help to give you a feel for the specific 'cycles' of astrology and the way they can subtly change your day-to-day life. For example, when you see the sign ☿, this means that the planet Mercury is retrograde at that time. Retrograde means it appears to be running backwards through the zodiac. Such a happening has a significant effect on communication skills, but this is only one small aspect of how the Personal Horoscope can help you.

With Your Personal Horoscope, the story doesn't end with the diary pages. It includes simple ways for you to work out which zodiac sign was occupied by the Moon at the time of your birth, and what this means for your personality. In addition, if you know the time of day you were born, it is possible to discover your Ascendant, yet another important guide to your personal make-up and potential.

Many readers are interested in relationships and in knowing how well they get on with people of other astrological signs. You might also be interested in the way you appear to other people. If you are such a person, the section on Venus will be of particular interest. Despite the rapidly changing position of this planet, you can work out your Venus sign, and learn what bearing it will have on your life.

Using Your Personal Horoscope, you can travel on one of the most fascinating and rewarding journeys that anyone can take – the journey to a better realisation of self.

7

THE ESSENCE OF VIRGO

Exploring the Personality of Virgo the Virgin

(24TH AUGUST–23RD SEPTEMBER)

What's in a sign?

Virgo people tend to be a rather extraordinary sort of mixture. Your ruling planet is Mercury, which makes you inclined to be rather chatty and quite sociable. On the other hand, yours is known as an Earth-ruled zodiac sign, which is usually steady and sometimes quite reserved. Thus, from the start, there are opposing energies ruling your life. This is not a problem when the right sort of balance is achieved and that is what you are looking for all the time. Repressed social and personal communication can make you worrisome, which in turn leads to a slightly fussy tendency that is not your most endearing quality.

At best you are quite ingenious and can usually rely on your strong intuition when weighing up the pros and cons of any given situation. Like all Earth signs you are able to accrue wealth and work hard to achieve your ultimate objectives in life. However, one is left with the impression that problems arise for Virgo when acquisition takes over. In other words, you need to relax more and to enjoy the fruits of your successes on a more regular basis.

Tidiness is important to you, and not just around your home. You particularly don't like loose ends and can be meticulous in your sense of detail. It seems likely that the fictional Sherlock Holmes was a Virgo subject and his ability to get to the absolute root of all situations is a stock-in-trade for the sign of the Virgin. Flexibility is especially important in relationships and you shouldn't become so obsessed with the way surroundings look that you fail to make the most of social opportunities.

Another tendency for Virgo is a need to 'keep up with the Joneses'. Why do you do this? Mainly because, like your fellow Mercury-ruled sign of Gemini, you haven't really as much confidence as seems to be the case. As a result you want to know that you are as good as anyone else, and if possible, better. This can, on occasion, lead to a sort of subconscious race that you can never hope to win. Learn to relax, and to recognise when you are on top anyway, and you are really motoring.

Virgo resources

Virgoan people are not at all short of savvy, and one of the most important considerations about your make-up is that you usually know how to proceed in a practical sense. At your disposal you have an armoury of weapons that can lead to a successful sort of life, especially in a practical and financial sense.

Your ruling planet, Mercury, makes you a good communicator and shows you the way to get on-side with the world at large. This quality means that you are rarely short of the right sort of information that is necessary in order to get things right first time. Where this doesn't prove to be possible you have Earth-sign tenacity, and an ability to work extremely hard for long hours in order to achieve your intended objectives. On the way, you tend on the whole to make friends, though you might find it hard to get through life without picking up one or two adversaries too.

Virgo people are capable of being gregarious and gossipy, whilst at the same time retaining an internal discipline which more perceptive people are inclined to recognise instinctively. You cement secure friendships and that means nearly always having someone to rely on in times of difficulty. But this isn't a one-way street, because you are a very supportive type yourself and would fight tenaciously on behalf of a person or a cause that you supported wholeheartedly. At such times you can appear to be quite brave, even though you could be quaking inside.

A tendency towards being nervy is not always as evident as you might think, mainly because you have the power and ability to keep it behind closed doors. Retaining the secrets of friends, despite your tendency to indulge in gossip, is an important part of your character and is the reason that others learn to trust you. Organisational skills are good and you love to sort out the puzzles of life, which makes you ideal for tedious jobs that many other people would find impossible to complete. Your curiosity knows no bounds and you would go to almost any length to answer questions that are uppermost in your mind at any point in time.

Beneath the surface

So what are you really like? Well, in the case of Virgo this might be the most interesting journey of all, and one that could deeply surprise even some of those people who think they know you very well indeed. First of all it must be remembered that your ruling planet is Mercury, known as the lord of communication. As a result it's important for you to keep in touch with the world at large. That's fine, except for the fact that your Earth-sign tendencies are inclined to make you basically quiet by nature.

Here we find something of a contradiction and one that leads to more than a few misunderstandings. You are particularly sensitive to little changes out there in the cosmos and so can be much more voluble on some days than on others. The result can be that others see you as being somewhat moody, which isn't really the case at all. You are inclined to be fairly nervy and would rarely be quite as confident as you give the impression of being. Although usually robust in terms of general health, this isn't always the case and a tendency towards a slightly hypochondriac nature can be the result. Some Virgoans can make an art form out of believing that they are unwell and you need to understand that part of the reason for this lies in your desire for attention.

Another accusation that is levelled at Virgoans is that they are inclined to be fussy over details. This is also an expression of your lack of basic confidence in yourself. For some reason you subconsciously assume that if every last matter is dealt with absolutely, all will work out well. In reality, the more relaxed you remain, the better you find your ability to cope with everyday life.

The simple truth is that you are much more capable than your inner nature tends to believe and could easily think more of yourself than you do. You have a logical mind, but also gain from the intuition that is possessed by all Mercury-ruled individuals. The more instinctive you become, the less you worry about things and the more relaxed life can seem to be. You also need to override a natural suspicion of those around you. Trust is a hard thing for you, but a very important one.

Making the best of yourself

There are many ways in which you can exploit the best potentials of your zodiac sign, and at the same time play down some of the less favourable possibilities. From the very start it's important to realise that the main criticism that comes your way from the outside world is that you are too fussy by half. So, simply avoid being critical of others and the way they do things. By all means stick to your own opinions, but avoid forcing them onto other people. If you can get over this hurdle, your personal popularity will already be that much greater. If people love you, you care for them in return – it's as simple as that, because at heart you aren't really very complicated.

Despite the fact that a little humility would go a long way, you also do need to remain sure of yourself. There's no real problem in allowing others their say, while following your own opinions all the same. Use your practical skills to the full and don't rush things just because other people seem to do so. Although you are ruled by quick Mercury, you also come from an Earth sign, which means steady progress.

Find outlets to desensitise your over-nervy nature. You can do this with plenty of healthy exercise and by taking an interest in subject matter that isn't of any great importance, but which you find appealing all the same. Avoid concentrating too much on any one thing, because that is the road to paranoia.

Realise that you have an innate sense of what is right, and that if it is utilised in the right way you can make gains for yourself and for the people you love. You have a good fund of ideas, so don't be afraid to use them. Most important of all, you need to remain confident but flexible. That's the path to popularity – something you need much more than you might realise.

The impressions you give

This can be something of a problem area to at least some people born under the zodiac sign of Virgo. There isn't much doubt that your heart is in the right place, and this fact isn't lost on many observers. All the same, you can appear to be very definite in your opinions, in fact to the point of stubbornness, and you won't give ground when you know you are in the right. A slight problem here might be that Virgoans nearly always think they have the moral and factual high ground. In the majority of cases this may indeed be true, but there are ways and means of putting the message across.

What Virgo needs more than anything else is tact. A combination of Mercury ruling your means of communication, and your Earth-sign heritage can, on occasions, make you appear to be rather blunt. Mercury also aids quick thinking and problem solving. The sum total can make it appear that you don't take other people's opinions into account and that you are prepared to railroad your ideas through if necessary.

Most people recognise that you are very capable, and may therefore automatically turn to you for leadership. It isn't certain how you will react under any given circumstance because although you can criticise others, your Earth-sign proclivities don't make you a natural leader. In a strong supportive role you can be wonderful and it is towards this scenario that you might choose to look.

Avoid people accusing you of being fussy by deliberately cultivating flexibility in your thinking and your actions. You are one of the kindest and most capable people to be found anywhere in the zodiac. All you need to do to complete the picture is to let the world at large know what you are. With your natural kindness and your ability to get things done, you can show yourself to be a really attractive individual. Look towards a brush-up of your public persona. Deep inside you are organised and caring, though a little nervy. Let people know exactly what you are – it only makes you more human.

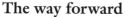

The way forward

Before anyone can move forward into anything, it is important for them to realise exactly where they are now. In your case this is especially true. Probably the most problematic area of Virgo is in understanding not what is being done but rather why. It is the inability to ask this question on a regular basis that leads Virgo into a rut now and again. Habit isn't simply a word to many people born under the zodiac sign of Virgo, it's a religion. The strange thing about this fact is that if you find yourself catapulted, against your will, into a different sort of routine, you soon learn to adopt it as if it were second nature. In other words this way of behaving is endemic, but not necessarily inevitable. The way out of it is simple and comes thanks to your ruling planet of Mercury. Keep talking, and at the same time listen. Adapt your life on a regular basis and say, 'So many habits are not necessary' at least ten times a day.

All the same it wouldn't be very prudent to throw out the baby with the bath water. Your ability to stick at things is justifiably legendary. This generally means that you arrive at your desired destination in life, even though it might take you a long time to get there. The usual result is respect from people who don't have your persistence or tenacity.

With regard to love and affection you are in a good position to place a protecting blanket around those you love the most. This is fine, as long as you check regularly that you are not suffocating them with it. If you allow a certain degree of freedom, people will respect your concern all the more and they won't fight against it. By all means communicate your affection and don't allow your natural Earth-sign reserve to get in the way of expressing feelings that are quite definite internally. This is another aspect of letting the world know what you are really like and is of crucial importance to your zodiac sign.

You need variety, and if possible an absence of worry. Only when things are going wrong do Virgoans become the fussy individuals that sometimes attract a little criticism. As long as you feel that you are in charge of your own destiny, you can remain optimistic – another vital requisite for Virgo. With just a little effort you can be one of the most popular and loved people around. Add to this your natural ability to succeed and the prognosis for the sign of the Virgin is very good.

VIRGO ON THE CUSP

Astrological profiles are altered for those people born at either the beginning or the end of a zodiac sign, or, more properly, on the cusps of a sign. In the case of Leo this would be on the 24th of August and for two or three days after, and similarly for Libra at the end of the sign, probably from the 21st to the 23rd of September.

The Leo Cusp – August 24th to 26th

If anything is designed to lighten the load of being a Virgoan, it's having a Leo quality in the nature too. All Virgoans are inclined to take themselves too seriously on occasions and they don't have half as much self-esteem as they could really use effectively. Being born on the Leo cusp gives better self-confidence, less of the supreme depths which Virgo alone can display and a much more superficial view of many aspects of life. The material success for which Virgo is famous probably won't be lacking, but there will also be a determination to have fun and let the bright, aspiring qualities that are so popular in the Leo character show.

In matters of love, you are likely to be easy-going, bright, bubbly and always willing to have a laugh. You relish good company, and though you sometimes go at things like a bull at a gate, your intentions are true and you know how to get others to like you a great deal. Family matters are right up your street, because not only do you have the ability to put down firm and enduring roots, but you are the most staunch and loyal protector of family values that anyone could wish for.

When it comes to working, you seem to have the best combination of all. You have the ability to work long and hard, achieving your objectives as all Virgoans do, but managing to do so with a smile permanently fixed to your face. You are naturally likely to find yourself at the head of things, where your combination of skills is going to be of the greatest use. This sign combination is to be found in every nook and cranny of the working world but perhaps less frequently in jobs which involve getting your hands dirty.

There are times when you definitely live on your nerves and when you don't get the genuine relaxation that the Virgoan qualities within you demand. Chances are you are much more robust than you consider yourself to be, and as long as you keep busy most of the time you tend to enjoy a contented life. The balance usually works well, because Leo lifts Virgo, whilst Virgo stabilises an often too superficial Lion.

The Libra Cusp – September 21st to 23rd

Virgo responds well to input from other parts of the zodiac and probably never more so than in the case of the Libran cusp. The reasons for this are very simple: what Virgo on its own lacks, Libra possesses, and it's the same on the other side of the coin. Libra is often flighty and doesn't take enough time to rest, but it is compensated by the balance inherent in the sign, so it weighs things carefully. Virgo on the other hand is deep and sometimes dark, but because it's ruled by capricious little Mercury, it can also be rather too impetuous. The potential break-even point is obvious and usually leads to a fairly easy-going individual, who is intellectual, thoughtful and practical when necessary.

You are a great person to have around in good times and bad, and you know how to have fun. A staunch support and helper to your friends, you enjoy a high degree of popularity, which usually extends to affairs of the heart. There may be more than one of these in your life and it's best for people born on this cusp not to marry in haste or too early in life. But even if you get things wrong first time around, you have the ability to bounce back quickly and don't become easily discouraged. It is good for you to be often in the company of gregarious and interesting people, but you are quite capable of surviving on your own when you have to.

Health matters may be on your mind more than is strictly necessary, and it's true that you can sometimes worry yourself into minor ailments that would not otherwise have existed. It is important for you to get plenty of rest and also to enjoy yourself. The more you work on behalf of others, the less time you spend thinking about your own possible ailments. Anxiety needs to be avoided, often by getting to the root of a problem and solving it quickly.

A capable and committed worker, you are at your best when able to share the decisions, but you are quite reliable when you have to make up your mind alone. You would never bully those beneath you. You are never short of support and you bring joy to life most of the time.

VIRGO AND ITS ASCENDANTS

The nature of every individual on the planet is composed of the rich variety of zodiac signs and planetary positions that were present at the time of their birth. Your Sun sign, which in your case is Virgo, is one of the many factors when it comes to assessing the unique person you are. Probably the most important consideration, other than your Sun sign, is to establish the zodiac sign that was rising over the eastern horizon at the time that you were born. This is your Ascending or Rising sign. Most popular astrology fails to take account of the Ascendant, and yet its importance remains with you from the very moment of your birth, through every day of your life. The Ascendant is evident in the way you approach the world, and so, when meeting a person for the first time, it is this astrological influence that you are most likely to notice first. Our Ascending sign essentially represents what we appear to be, while the Sun sign is what we feel inside ourselves.

The Ascendant also has the potential for modifying our overall nature. For example, if you were born at a time of day when Virgo was passing over the eastern horizon (this would be around the time of dawn) then you would be classed as a double Virgo. As such, you would typify this zodiac sign, both internally and in your dealings with others. However, if your Ascendant sign turned out to be a Fire sign, such as Aries, there would be a profound alteration of nature, away from the expected qualities of Virgo.

One of the reasons why popular astrology often ignores the Ascendant is that it has always been rather difficult to establish. We have found a way to make this possible by devising an easy-to-use table, which you will find on page 157 of this book. Using this, you can establish your Ascendant sign at a glance. You will need to know your rough time of birth, then it is simply a case of following the instructions.

For those readers who have no idea of their time of birth it might be worth allowing a good friend, or perhaps your partner, to read through the section that follows this introduction. Someone who deals with you on a regular basis may easily discover your Ascending sign, even though you could have some difficulty establishing it for yourself. A good understanding of this component of your nature is essential if you want to be aware of that 'other person' who is responsible for the way you make contact with the world at large. Your Sun sign, Ascendant sign, and the other pointers in this book will, together, allow you a far better understanding of what makes you tick as an individual. Peeling back the different layers of your astrological make-up can be an enlightening experience, and the Ascendant may represent one of the most important layers of all.

Virgo with Virgo Ascendant

You get the best of both worlds, and on rare occasions the worst too. Frighteningly efficient, you have the ability to scare people with your constant knack of getting it right. This won't endear you to everyone, particularly those who pride themselves on being disorganised. You make a loyal friend and would do almost anything for someone who is important to you, though you do so in a quiet way because you are not the most noisy of types. Chances are that you possess the ability to write well and you also have a cultured means of verbal communication on those occasions when you really choose to speak out.

It isn't difficult for you to argue your case, though much of the time you refuse to do so and can lock yourself into your own private world for days on end. If you are at ease with yourself you possess a powerful personality, which you can express well. Conversely, you can live on your nerves and cause problems for yourself. Meditation is good, fussing over details that really don't matter at all is less useful. Once you have chosen a particular course of action there are few people around with sufficient will-power to prevent you from getting what you want. Wide open spaces where the hand of nature is all around can make you feel very relaxed.

Virgo with Libra Ascendant

Libra has the ability to lighten almost any load and it is particularly good at doing so when it is brought together with the much more repressed sign of Virgo. To the world at large you seem relaxed, happy and able to cope with most of the pressures that life places upon you. Not only do you deal with your own life in a bright and breezy manner but you are usually on hand to help others out of any dilemma that they might make for themselves. With excellent powers of communication you leave the world at large in no doubt whatsoever concerning both your opinions and your wishes. It is in the talking stakes that you really excel because Virgo brings the silver tongue of Mercury and Libra adds the Air-sign desire to be in constant touch with the world outside your door.

You like to have a good time and are often found in the company of interesting and stimulating people, who have the ability to bring out the very best in your bright and sparkling personality. Underneath however, there is still much of the worrying Virgoan to be found and this means that you have to learn to relax inside as well as appearing to do so externally. In fact you are much more complex than most people would realise and definitely would not be suited to a life that allowed you too much time to think about yourself.

Virgo with Scorpio Ascendant

This is intensity carried through to the absolute. If you have a problem, it is that you fail to externalise all that is going on inside that deep, bubbling cauldron of your inner self. Realising what you are capable of is not a problems only start when you have to make it plain to those around you what you want. Part of the reason for this is that you don't always understand yourself. You love intensely and would do absolutely anything for a person you are fond of, even though you might have to inconvenience yourself a great deal on the way. Relationships can cause you slight problems however, since you need to associate with people who at least come somewhere near to understanding what makes you tick. If you manage to bridge the gap between yourself and the world, you show yourself to be powerful, magnetic and compulsive.

There are times when you definitely prefer to stay quiet though you do have a powerful ability to get your message across when you think it is necessary to do so. There are people around who might think that you are a push-over but they could easily get a shock when you sense that the time is right to answer back. You probably have a very orderly house and don't care for clutter of any sort.

Virgo with Sagittarius Ascendant

This is a combination that might look rather odd at first sight because these two signs have so very little in common. However the saying goes that opposites attract and in terms of the personality you display to the world this is especially true. Not everyone understands what makes you tick but you try to show the least complicated face to the world that you can manage to display. You can be deep and secretive on occasions, and yet at other times you can start talking as soon as you climb out of bed and never stop until you are back there again. Inspirational and spontaneous, you take the world by storm on those occasions when you are free from worries and firing on all cylinders. It is a fact that you support your friends, though there are rather more of them than would be the case for Virgo taken on its own and you don't always choose them as wisely as you might.

There are times when you display a temper and although Sagittarius is incapable of bearing a grudge, the same cannot be said for Virgo, which has a better memory than the elephant. For the best results in life you need to relax as much as possible and avoid overheating that powerful and busy brain. Virgo gives you the ability to concentrate on one thing at once, a skill you should encourage.

Virgo with Capricorn Ascendant

Your endurance, persistence and concentration are legendary and there is virtually nothing that eludes you once you have the bit between your teeth. You are not the pushy, fussy, go-getting sort of Virgoan but are steady, methodical and very careful. Once you have made up your mind, a whole team of wild horses could not change it and although this can be a distinct blessing at times, it is a quality that can bring odd problems into your life too. The difficulty starts when you adopt a lost or less than sensible cause. Even in the face of overwhelming evidence that you are wrong there is something inside you that prevents any sort of U-turn and so you walk forward as solidly as only you are able, to a destination that won't suit you at all.

There are few people around who are more loyal and constant than you can be. There is a lighter and brighter side to your nature and the one or two people who are most important in your life will know how to bring it out. You have a wicked sense of humour, particularly if you have had a drink or when you are feeling on top form. Travel does you the world of good, even if there is a part of you that would rather stay at home. You have a potent, powerful and magnetic personality but for much of the time it is kept carefully hidden.

Virgo with Aquarius Ascendant

How could anyone make convention unconventional? Well, if anyone can manage, you can. There are great contradictions here because on the one hand you always want to do what is expected, but the Aquarian quality within your nature loves to surprise everyone on the way. If you don't always know what you are thinking or doing, it's a pretty safe bet that others won't either, so it's important on occasions to stop and really think. However this is not a pressing concern because you tend to live a fairly happy life and muddle through no matter what. Other people tend to take to you well and it is likely that you will have many friends. You tend to be bright and cheerful and can approach even difficult tasks with the certainty that you have the skills necessary to see them through to their conclusion. Give and take are important factors in the life of any individual and particularly so in your case. Because you can stretch yourself in order to understand what makes other people think and act in the way that they do, you have the reputation of being a good friend and a reliable colleague.

In love you can be somewhat more fickle than the typical Virgoan and yet you are always interesting to live with. Where you are, things happen, and you mix a sparkling wit with deep insights.

Virgo with Pisces Ascendant

You might have been accused on occasions of being too sensitive for your own good, a charge that is not entirely without foundation. Certainly you are very understanding of the needs of others, sometimes to the extent that you put everything aside to help them. This would also be true in the case of charities, for you care very much about the world and the people who cling tenaciously to its surface. Your ability to love on a one-to-one basis knows no bounds though you may not discriminate as much as you could, particularly when young, and might have one or two false starts in the love stakes. You don't always choose to verbalise your thoughts and this can cause problems, because there is always so much going on in your mind and Virgo especially needs good powers of communication. Pisces is quieter and you need to force yourself to say what you think when the explanation is important.

You would never betray a confidence and sometimes take on rather more for the sake of your friends than is strictly good for you. This is not a fault but can cause you problems all the same. Because you are so intuitive there is little that escapes your attention, though you should avoid being pessimistic about your insights. Changes of scenery suit you and extensive travel would bring out the best in what can be a repressed nature at times.

Virgo with Aries Ascendant

Virgo is steady and sure, though also fussy and stubborn. Aries is fast and determined, restless and active. It can be seen already that this is a rather strange meeting of characteristics and because Virgo is ruled by capricious Mercury, the result will change from hour to hour and day to day. It isn't merely that others find it difficult to know where they are with you; they can't even understand what makes you tick. This will make you the subject of endless fascination and attention, at which you will be apparently surprised but inwardly pleased. If anyone ever really gets to know what goes on in that busy mind they may find the implications very difficult to deal with and it is a fact that only you would have the ability to live inside your crowded head.

As a partner and a parent you are second to none, though you tend to get on better with your children once they start to grow, since by this time you may be slightly less restricting to their own desires, which will often clash with your own. You are capable of give and take and could certainly not be considered selfish, though your desire to get the best from everyone might be misconstrued on occasion.

Virgo with Taurus Ascendant

This combination tends to amplify the Taurean qualities that you naturally possess and this is the case because both Taurus and Virgo are Earth signs. However, there are certain factors related to Virgo that show themselves very differently than the sign's cousin Taurus. Virgo is more fussy, nervy and pedantic than Taurus, and all of these qualities are going to show up in your nature at one level or another. On the plus side you might be slightly less concerned about having a perfect home and a perfect family, and your interest in life appears at a more direct level than that of the true Taurean. You care very much about your home and family and are very loyal to your friends. It's true that you sometimes tend to try and take them over and you can also show a marked tendency to dominate, but your heart is in the right place and most people recognise that your caring is genuine.

One problem is that there are very few shades of grey in your life, which is certainly not the case for other zodiac sign combinations. Living your life in the way that you do there isn't much room for compromise and this fact alone can prove to be something of a problem where relationships are concerned. In a personal sense you need a partner who is willing to be organised and one who relies on your judgements, which don't change all that often.

Virgo with Gemini Ascendant

A Gemini Ascendant means that you are ruled by Mercury, both through your Sun sign and through the sign that was rising at the time of your birth. This means that words are your basic tools in life and you use them to the full. Some writers have this combination, because even speaking to people virtually all the time is not enough. Although you have many friends you are fairly high-minded, which means that you can make enemies too. The fact is that people either care very much for you, or else they don't like you at all. This can be difficult for you to come to terms with because you don't really set out to cause friction – it simply attracts itself to you.

Although you love travel, home is important too and there is a basic insecurity in your nature that comes about as a result of an overdose of Mercury, which makes you nervy and sometimes far less confident than anyone would guess. Success in your life may be slower arriving with this combination because you are determined to achieve your objectives on your own terms and this can take time. Always a contradiction, often a puzzle to others, your ultimate happiness in life is directly proportional to the effort you put in, though this should not mean wearing yourself out on the way.

Virgo with Cancer Ascendant

What can this union of zodiac signs bring to the party that isn't there in either Virgo or Cancer alone? Well quite a bit actually. Virgo can be very fussy on occasions and too careful for its own good. The presence of steady, serene Cancer alters the perspectives and allows a smoother, more flowing Virgoan to greet the world. You are chatty, easy to know and exhibit a combination of the practical skills of Virgo, together with the deep and penetrating insights that are typical of Cancer. This can make you appear to be very powerful, and your insights are second to none. You are a born organiser and love to be where things are happening, even if you are only there to help make the sandwiches or to pour the tea. Invariably your role will be much greater but you don't seek personal acclaim and are a good team player on most occasions.

There is a quiet side to your nature and those who live with you will eventually get used to your need for solitude. This seems strange because Virgo is generally such a chatterbox and, taken on its own, is rarely quiet for long. In love you show great affection and a sense of responsibility that makes you an ideal parent, though it is possible sometimes that you care rather more than you are willing to show.

Virgo with Leo Ascendant

Here we have cheerfulness allied to efficiency, which can be a very positive combination most of the time. With all the sense of honour, justice and bravery of the Leo subject, Virgo adds staying power through tedious situations and offers you a slightly more serious view of life than we would expect from the Lion alone. In almost any situation you can keep going until you get to your chosen destination and you also find the time to reach out to the people who need your unique nature the most. Few would deny your kindness, though you can attract a little envy because it seems as though yours is the sort of personality that everyone else wants.

Most people born with this combination have a radiant smile and will do their best to think situations through carefully. If there is a tendency to be foolhardy, it is carefully masked beneath a covering of Virgoan common sense. Family matters are dealt with efficiently and with great love. Some might see you as close one moment and distant the next. The truth is that you are always on the go and have a thousand different things to think about, all at the same time. On the whole your presence is noticed and you may represent the most loyal friend of them all.

THE MOON AND THE PART IT PLAYS IN YOUR LIFE

In astrology, the Moon is probably the single most important heavenly body after the Sun. Its unique position, as partner to the Earth on its journey around the solar system, means that the Moon appears to pass through the signs of the zodiac extremely quickly. The zodiac position of the Moon at the time of your birth plays a great part in your personality and is especially significant in the build-up of your emotional nature.

Your Own Moon Sign

Discovering the position of the Moon at the time of your birth has always been notoriously difficult, because tracking the complex zodiac positions of the Moon is not easy. This process has been reduced to three simple stages with our Lunar Tables. A breakdown of the Moon's zodiac positions can be found from page 33 onwards, so that once you know what your Moon Sign is, you can see what part this plays in the overall build-up of your personal character.

If you follow the instructions on the next page you will soon be able to work out exactly what zodiac sign the Moon occupied on the day that you were born and you can then go on to compare the reading for this position with those of your Sun sign and your Ascendant. It is partly the comparison between these three important positions that goes towards making you the unique individual you are.

HOW TO DISCOVER YOUR MOON SIGN

This is a three-stage process. You may need a pen and a piece of paper but if you follow the instructions below the process should only take a minute or so.

STAGE 1 First of all you need to know the Moon Age at the time of your birth. If you look at Moon Table 1, on page 33, you will find all the years between 1918 and 2016 down the left side. Find the year of your birth and then trace across to the right to the month of your birth. Where the two intersect you will find a number. This is the date of the New Moon in the month that you were born. You now need to count forward the number of days between the New Moon and your own birthday. For example, if the New Moon in the month of your birth was shown as being the 6th and you were born on the 20th, your Moon Age Day would be 14. If the New Moon in the month of your birth came after your birthday, you need to count forward from the New Moon in the previous month. Whatever the result, jot this number down so that you do not forget it.

STAGE 2 Take a look at Moon Table 2 on page 34. Down the left-hand column look for the date of your birth. Now trace across to the month of your birth. Where the two meet you will find a letter. Copy this letter down alongside your Moon Age Day.

STAGE 3 Moon Table 3 on page 34 will supply you with the zodiac sign the Moon occupied on the day of your birth. Look for your Moon Age Day down the left hand column and then for the letter you found in Stage 2. Where the two converge you will find a zodiac sign and this is the sign occupied by the Moon on the day that you were born.

Your Zodiac Moon Sign Explained

You will find a profile of all zodiac Moon Signs on pages 35 to 38, showing in yet another way how astrology can be used to explain the individual that you are. In each daily entry of the Astral Diary you can find the zodiac position of the Moon for every day of the year. This also allows you to discover your lunar birthdays. Since the Moon passes through all the signs of the zodiac in about a month, you can expect something like twelve lunar birthdays each year. At these times you are likely to be emotionally steady and able to make the sort of decisions that have real, lasting value.

MOON TABLE 1

YEAR	JUL	AUG	SEP	YEAR	JUL	AUG	SEP	YEAR	JUL	AUG	SEP
1918	8	6	4	1951	4	2	1	1984	28	26	25
1919	27	25	23	1952	23	20	19	1985	17	16	14
1920	15	14	12	1953	11	9	8	1986	7	5	4
1921	5	3	2	1954	29	28	27	1987	25	24	23
1922	24	22	21	1955	19	17	16	1988	13	12	11
1923	14	12	10	1956	8	6	4	1989	3	1/31	29
1924	2/31	30	28	1957	27	25	23	1990	22	20	19
1925	20	19	18	1958	16	15	13	1991	11	9	8
1926	9	8	7	1959	6	4	3	1992	29	28	26
1927	28	27	25	1960	24	22	21	1993	19	17	16
1928	17	16	14	1961	12	11	10	1994	8	7	5
1929	6	5	3	1962	1/31	30	28	1995	27	26	24
1930	25	24	22	1963	20	19	17	1996	15	14	13
1931	15	13	12	1964	9	7	6	1997	4	3	2
1932	3	2/31	30	1965	28	26	25	1998	23	22	20
1933	22	21	19	1966	17	16	14	1999	13	11	10
1934	11	10	9	1967	7	5	4	2000	1/31	29	27
1935	30	29	27	1968	25	24	23	2001	20	19	17
1936	18	17	15	1969	13	12	11	2002	9	8	6
1937	8	6	4	1970	4	2	1	2003	28	27	26
1938	27	25	23	1971	22	20	19	2004	16	14	13
1939	16	15	13	1972	11	9	8	2005	6	4	3
1940	5	4	2	1973	29	28	27	2006	25	23	22
1941	24	22	21	1974	19	17	16	2007	15	13	12
1942	13	12	10	1975	9	7	5	2008	31	31	30
1943	2	1/30	29	1976	27	25	23	2009	22	20	19
1944	20	18	17	1977	16	14	13	2010	12	10	8
1945	9	8	6	1978	5	4	2	2011	2/31	29	27
1946	28	26	25	1979	24	22	21	2012	19	17	16
1947	17	16	14	1980	12	11	10	2013	7	6	4
1948	6	5	3	1981	1/31	29	28	2014	25	24	23
1949	25	24	23	1982	20	19	17	2015	16	15	13
1950	15	13	12	1983	10	8	7	2016	4	2	1

TABLE 2   MOON TABLE 3

DAY	AUG	SEP	M/D	U	V	W	X	Y	Z	a
1	U	X	0	LE	LE	LE	VI	VI	LI	LI
2	U	X	1	LE	VI	VI	VI	LI	LI	LI
3	V	X	2	VI	VI	VI	LI	LI	LI	LI
4	V	Y	3	VI	VI	LI	LI	LI	SC	SC
5	V	Y	4	LI	LI	LI	LI	SC	SC	SC
6	V	Y	5	LI	LI	SC	SC	SC	SC	SA
7	V	Y	6	LI	SC	SC	SC	SA	SA	SA
8	V	Y	7	SC	SC	SA	SA	SA	SA	SA
9	V	Y	8	SC	SC	SA	SA	SA	CP	CP
10	V	Y	9	SA	SA	SA	SA	CP	CP	CP
11	V	Y	10	SA	SA	CP	CP	CP	CP	AQ
12	V	Y	11	CP	CP	CP	CP	AQ	AQ	AQ
13	V	Y	12	CP	CP	AQ	AQ	AQ	AQ	PI
14	W	Z	13	CP	CP	AQ	AQ	AQ	PI	PI
15	W	Z	14	AQ	AQ	PI	PI	PI	PI	AR
16	W	Z	15	AQ	AQ	PI	PI	PI	PI	AR
17	W	Z	16	AQ	PI	PI	PI	AR	AR	AR
18	W	Z	17	PI	PI	PI	AR	AR	AR	AR
19	W	Z	18	PI	PI	AR	AR	AR	AR	TA
20	W	Z	19	PI	AR	AR	AR	TA	TA	TA
21	W	Z	20	AR	AR	TA	TA	TA	TA	GE
22	W	Z	21	AR	TA	TA	TA	GE	GE	GE
23	W	Z	22	TA	TA	TA	GE	GE	GE	GE
24	X	a	23	TA	TA	GE	GE	GE	GE	CA
25	X	a	24	TA	GE	GE	GE	CA	CA	CA
26	X	a	25	GE	GE	CA	CA	CA	CA	CA
27	X	a	26	GE	CA	CA	CA	LE	LE	LE
28	X	a	27	CA	CA	CA	LE	LE	LE	LE
29	X	a	28	CA	CA	LE	LE	LE	LE	VI
30	X	a	29	CA	LE	LE	LE	VI	VI	VI
31	X	–								

AR = Aries, TA = Taurus, GE = Gemini, CA = Cancer, LE = Leo, VI = Virgo,
LI = Libra, SC = Scorpio, SA = Sagittarius, CP = Capricorn, AQ = Aquarius, PI = Pisces

MOON SIGNS

Moon in Aries

You have a strong imagination, courage, determination and a desire to do things in your own way and forge your own path through life.

Originality is a key attribute; you are seldom stuck for ideas although your mind is changeable and you should take the time to focus on individual tasks. Often quick tempered, you take orders from few people and live life at a fast pace. Avoid health problems by taking regular time out for rest and relaxation.

Emotionally, it is important that you talk to those you are closest to and work out your true feelings. Once you discover that people are there to help, there is less necessity for you to do everything yourself.

Moon in Taurus

The Moon in Taurus gives you a courteous and friendly manner, which means you are likely to have many friends.

The good things in life mean a lot to you, as Taurus is an Earth sign that delights in experiences which please the senses. Hence you are probably a lover of good food and drink, which may in turn mean you need to keep an eye on the bathroom scales, especially as looking good is also important to you.

Emotionally you are fairly stable and you stick by your own standards. Taureans do not respond well to change. Intuition also plays an important part in your life.

Moon in Gemini

You have a warm-hearted character, sympathetic and eager to help others. At times reserved, you can also be articulate and chatty: this is part of the paradox of Gemini, which always brings duplicity to someone's nature. You are interested in current affairs, have a good intellect, and are good company and likely to have many friends. Most of your friends have a high opinion of you and would be ready to defend you should the need arise. However, this is usually unnecessary, as you are quite capable of defending yourself in any verbal confrontation.

Travel is important to your inquisitive mind and you find intellectual stimulus in mixing with people from different cultures. You also gain much from reading, writing and the arts but you do need plenty of rest and relaxation in order to avoid fatigue.

Moon in Cancer

The Moon in Cancer at the time of birth is a fortunate position as Cancer is the Moon's natural home. This means that the qualities of compassion and understanding given by the Moon are especially enhanced in your nature, and you are friendly and sociable and cope well with emotional pressures. You cherish home and family life, and happily do the domestic tasks. Your surroundings are important to you and you hate squalor and filth. You are likely to have a love of music and poetry.

Your basic character, although at times changeable like the Moon itself, depends on symmetry. You aim to make your surroundings comfortable and harmonious, for yourself and those close to you.

Moon in Leo

The best qualities of the Moon and Leo come together to make you warm-hearted, fair, ambitious and self-confident. With good organisational abilities, you invariably rise to a position of responsibility in your chosen career. This is fortunate as you don't enjoy being an 'also-ran' and would rather be an important part of a small organisation than a menial in a large one.

You should be lucky in love, and happy, provided you put in the effort to make a comfortable home for yourself and those close to you. It is likely that you will have a love of pleasure, sport, music and literature. Life brings you many rewards, most of them as a direct result of your own efforts, although you may be luckier than average and ready to make the best of any situation.

Moon in Virgo

You are endowed with good mental abilities and a keen receptive memory, but you are never ostentatious or pretentious. Naturally quite reserved, you still have many friends. Marital relationships must be discussed carefully and worked at so that they remain harmonious, as personal attachments can be a problem if you do not give them your full attention.

Talented and persevering, you possess artistic qualities and are a good homemaker. Earning your honours through genuine merit, you work long and hard towards your objectives but show little pride in your achievements. Many short journeys will be undertaken in your life.

Moon in Libra

With the Moon in Libra you are naturally popular and make friends easily. People like you, probably more than you realise, you bring fun to a party and are a natural diplomat. For all its good points, Libra is not the most stable of astrological signs and, as a result, your emotions can be a little unstable too. Therefore, although the Moon in Libra is said to be good for love and marriage, your Sun sign and Rising sign will have an important effect on your emotional and loving qualities.

You must remember to relate to others in your decision-making. Co-operation is crucial because Libra represents the 'balance' of life that can only be achieved through harmonious relationships. Conformity is not easy for you because Libra, an Air sign, likes its independence.

Moon in Scorpio

Some people might call you pushy. In fact, all you really want to do is to live life to the full and protect yourself and your family from the pressures of life. Take care to avoid giving the impression of being sarcastic or impulsive and use your energies wisely and constructively.

You have great courage and you invariably achieve your goals by force of personality and sheer effort. You are fond of mystery and are good at predicting the outcome of situations and events. Travel experiences can be beneficial to you.

You may experience problems if you do not take time to examine your motives in a relationship, and also if you allow jealousy, always a feature of Scorpio, to cloud your judgement.

Moon in Sagittarius

The Moon in Sagittarius helps to make you a generous individual with humanitarian qualities and a kind heart. Restlessness may be intrinsic as your mind is seldom still. Perhaps because of this, you have a need for change that could lead you to several major moves during your adult life. You are not afraid to stand your ground when you know your judgement is right, you speak directly and have good intuition.

At work you are quick, efficient and versatile and so you make an ideal employee. You need work to be intellectually demanding and do not enjoy tedious routines.

In relationships, you anger quickly if faced with stupidity or deception, though you are just as quick to forgive and forget. Emotionally, there are times when your heart rules your head.

Moon in Capricorn

The Moon in Capricorn makes you popular and likely to come into the public eye in some way. The watery Moon is not entirely comfortable in the Earth sign of Capricorn and this may lead to some difficulties in the early years of life. An initial lack of creative ability and indecision must be overcome before the true qualities of patience and perseverance inherent in Capricorn can show through.

You have good administrative ability and are a capable worker, and if you are careful you can accumulate wealth. But you must be cautious and take professional advice in partnerships, as you are open to deception. You may be interested in social or welfare work, which suit your organisational skills and sympathy for others.

Moon in Aquarius

The Moon in Aquarius makes you an active and agreeable person with a friendly, easy-going nature. Sympathetic to the needs of others, you flourish in a laid-back atmosphere. You are broad-minded, fair and open to suggestion, although sometimes you have an unconventional quality which others can find hard to understand.

You are interested in the strange and curious, and in old articles and places. You enjoy trips to these places and gain much from them. Political, scientific and educational work interests you and you might choose a career in science or technology.

Money-wise, you make gains through innovation and concentration and Lunar Aquarians often tackle more than one job at a time. In love you are kind and honest.

Moon in Pisces

You have a kind, sympathetic nature, somewhat retiring at times, but you always take account of others' feelings and help when you can.

Personal relationships may be problematic, but as life goes on you can learn from your experiences and develop a better understanding of yourself and the world around you.

You have a fondness for travel, appreciate beauty and harmony and hate disorder and strife. You may be fond of literature and would make a good writer or speaker yourself. You have a creative imagination and may come across as an incurable romantic. You have strong intuition, maybe bordering on a mediumistic quality, which sets you apart from the mass. You may not be rich in cash terms, but your personal gifts are worth more than gold.

VIRGO IN LOVE

Discover how compatible in love you are with people from the same and other signs of the zodiac. Five stars equals a match made in heaven!

Virgo meets Virgo

Unlike many same-sign combinations this is not a five-star pairing, for one very good reason. Virgo needs to react with other signs to reveal its hidden best side. Two Virgoans together, although enjoying some happiness, will not present a dynamic, sparkling and carefree appearance. They should run an efficient and financially sound household, but that all-important ingredient, passion, may be distinctly low-key. Star rating: ***

Virgo meets Libra

There have been some rare occasions when this match has found great success, but usually the inward-looking Virgoan depresses the naturally gregarious Libran. Libra appears self-confident but is not so beneath the surface and needs encouragement to develop inner confidence, which may not come from Virgo. Constancy can be a problem for Libra, who also tires easily and may find Virgo dull. A less serious approach from Virgo is needed to make this work. Star rating: **

Virgo meets Scorpio

There are one or two potential difficulties here, but there is also a meeting point from which to overcome them. Virgo is very caring and protective, a trait which Scorpio understands and even emulates. Both signs are consistent, but also sarcastic. Scorpio will impress Virgo with its serious side, and may also uncover a hidden passion in Virgo which all too often lies deep within its Earth-sign nature. Material success is very likely, with Virgo taking the lion's share of domestic chores and family responsibilities. Star rating: ***

Virgo meets Sagittarius

There can be some strange happenings in this relationship. Sagittarius and Virgo view life so differently there are always new discoveries. Virgo is much more of a home bird than Sagittarius, but that won't matter if the Archer introduces its hectic social life gradually. More importantly, Sagittarius understands that it takes Virgo a long time to free its hidden 'inner sprite', but once free it will be fun all the way – until Virgo's thrifty nature takes over. There are great possibilities, but effort is required. Star rating: ***

Virgo meets Capricorn

One of the best possible combinations, because Virgo and Capricorn have an instinctive understanding. Both signs know the value of dedicated hard work and apply it equally in a relationship and other areas of life. Two of the most practical signs, nothing is beyond them, even if to outsiders they appear rather sterile or lacking in 'oomph'. What matters most is that the individuals are happy, and with so much in common, the likelihood of mutual material success and a shared devotion to home and family, there isn't much doubt of that. Star rating: *****

Virgo meets Aquarius

Aquarius is a strange sign because no matter how well one knows it, it always manages to surprise, and for this reason, against the odds, it's quite likely that Aquarius will form a successful relationship with Virgo. Aquarius is changeable, unpredictable and often quite 'odd' while Virgo is steady, a fuss-pot and very practical. Herein lies the key. What one sign needs, the other provides and that may be the surest recipe for success imaginable. On-lookers may not know why the couple are happy, but they will recognise that this is the case. Star rating: ****

Virgo meets Pisces

This looks an unpromising match from beginning to end. There are exceptions to every rule, particularly where Pisces is concerned, but these two signs are both so deep it's hard to imagine that they could ever find what makes the other tick. Virgo's ruminations are extremely materialistic, while Pisces exists in a world of deep-felt, poorly expressed emotion. Pisces and Virgo might find they don't talk much, so only in a contemplative, almost monastic, match would they ever get on. Still, in a vast zodiac, anything is possible. Star rating: **

Virgo meets Aries

Neither of these signs really understands the other, and that could easily lead to a clash. Virgo is so pedantic, which will drive Aries up the wall, while Aries always wants to be moving on to the next objective before Virgo is even settled with the last one. It will take time for these two to get to know each other, but this is a great business matching. If a personal relationship is seen in these terms then the prognosis can be quite good, but on the whole, this is not an inspiring match. Star rating: ***

Virgo meets Taurus

This is a difficult basis for a successful relationship, and yet it often works. Both signs are from the Earth element, so have a common-sense approach to life. They have a mutual understanding, and share many interests. Taurus understands and copes well with Virgo's fussy nature, while Virgo revels in the Bull's tidy and artistic qualities. Both sides are committed to achieving lasting material success. There won't be fireworks, and the match may lack a certain 'spiritual' feel, but as that works both ways it may not be a problem. Star rating: *****

Virgo meets Gemini

The fact that both these signs are ruled by the planet Mercury might at first seem good but, unfortunately, Mercury works very differently in these signs. Gemini is untidy, flighty, quick, changeable and easily bored, while Virgo is fastidious, steady and constant. If Virgo is willing to accept some anarchy all can be well, but this not usually the case. Virgoans are deep thinkers and may find Gemini a little superficial. This pair can be compatible intellectually, though even this side isn't without its problems. Star rating: ***

Virgo meets Cancer

This match has little chance of success, for fairly simple reasons: Cancer's generous affection will be submerged by the Virgoan depths, not because Virgo is uncaring but because it expresses itself so differently. As both signs are naturally quiet, things might become a bit boring. They would be mutually supportive, possibly financially successful and have a very tidy house, but they won't share much sparkle, enthusiasm, risk-taking or passion. If this pair were stranded on a desert island, they might live at different ends of it. Star rating: **

Virgo meets Leo

There is a chance for this couple, but it won't be trouble-free. Leo and Virgo view life very differently: Virgo is of a serious nature and struggles to relate to Leo's relentless optimism and cheerfulness and can find it annoying. Leo, meanwhile, may find Virgo stodgy, sometimes dark and uninspiring. The saving grace comes through communication – Leo knows how to make Virgo talk, which is what it needs. If this pair find happiness, though, it may be a case of opposites attract! Star rating: ***

VENUS:
THE PLANET OF LOVE

If you look up at the sky around sunset or sunrise you will often see Venus in close attendance to the Sun. It is arguably one of the most beautiful sights of all and there is little wonder that historically it became associated with the goddess of love. But although Venus does play an important part in the way you view love and in the way others see you romantically, this is only one of the spheres of influence that it enjoys in your overall character.

Venus has a part to play in the more cultured side of your life and has much to do with your appreciation of art, literature, music and general creativity. Even the way you look is responsive to the part of the zodiac that Venus occupied at the start of your life, though this fact is also down to your Sun sign and Ascending sign. If, at the time you were born, Venus occupied one of the more gregarious zodiac signs, you will be more likely to wear your heart on your sleeve, as well as to be more attracted to entertainment, social gatherings and good company. If, on the other hand, Venus occupied a quiet zodiac sign at the time of your birth, you tend to be more retiring and less willing to take over in public situations.

It's good to know what part the planet Venus plays in your life for it can have a great bearing on the way you appear to the rest of the world. Since we all have to mix with others, you can learn to make the very best of what Venus has to offer you.

One of the great complications in the past has always been trying to establish exactly what zodiac position Venus enjoyed when you were born, because the planet is notoriously difficult to track. However, we have solved that problem by creating a table that is exclusive to your Sun sign, which you will find on the following page.

Establishing your Venus sign could not be easier. Just look up the year of your birth on the next page and you will see a sign of the Zodiac. This was the sign that Venus occupied in the period covered by your sign in that year. If Venus occupied more than one sign during the period, this is indicated by the date on which the sign changed, and the name of the new sign. For instance, if you were born in 1950, Venus was in Leo until the 10th September, after which time it was in Virgo. If you were born before 10th September your Venus sign is Leo, if you were born on or after 10th September, your Venus sign is Virgo. Once you have established the position of Venus at the time of your birth, you can then look in the pages which follow to see how this has a bearing on your life as a whole.

1918 LEO / 12.9 VIRGO
1919 VIRGO
1920 VIRGO / 5.9 LIBRA
1921 CANCER / 31.8 LEO
1922 LIBRA / 8.9 SCORPIO
1923 LEO / 28.8 VIRGO /
    20.9 LIBRA
1924 CANCER / 9.9 LEO
1925 LIBRA / 16.9 SCORPIO
1926 LEO / 12.9 VIRGO
1927 VIRGO
1928 VIRGO / 5.9 LIBRA
1929 CANCER / 31.8 LEO
1930 LIBRA / 7.9 SCORPIO
1931 LEO / 28.8 VIRGO /
    20.9 LIBRA
1932 CANCER / 9.9 LEO
1933 LIBRA / 16.9 SCORPIO
1934 LEO / 11.9 VIRGO
1935 VIRGO
1936 VIRGO / 4.9 LIBRA
1937 CANCER / 31.8 LEO
1938 LIBRA / 7.9 SCORPIO
1939 LEO / 27.8 VIRGO /
    19.9 LIBRA
1940 CANCER / 9.9 LEO
1941 LIBRA / 15.9 SCORPIO
1942 LEO / 11.9 VIRGO
1943 VIRGO
1944 VIRGO / 4.9 LIBRA
1945 CANCER / 30.8 LEO
1946 LIBRA / 7.9 SCORPIO
1947 LEO / 27.8 VIRGO /
    18.9 LIBRA
1948 CANCER / 9.9 LEO
1949 LIBRA / 15.9 SCORPIO
1950 LEO / 10.9 VIRGO
1951 VIRGO
1952 VIRGO / 3.9 LIBRA
1953 CANCER / 30.8 LEO
1954 LIBRA / 7.9 SCORPIO
1955 LEO / 26.8 VIRGO /
    17.9 LIBRA
1956 CANCER / 8.9 LEO
1957 LIBRA / 15.9 SCORPIO
1958 LEO / 10.9 VIRGO
1959 VIRGO / 20.9 LEO
1960 VIRGO / 3.9 LIBRA
1961 CANCER / 30.8 LEO
1962 LIBRA / 8.9 SCORPIO
1963 LEO / 26.8 VIRGO /
    17.9 LIBRA
1964 CANCER / 8.9 LEO
1965 LIBRA / 15.9 SCORPIO

1966 LEO / 9.9 VIRGO
1967 VIRGO / 10.9 LEO
1968 VIRGO / 2.9 LIBRA
1969 CANCER / 29.8 LEO
1970 LIBRA / 8.9 SCORPIO
1971 LEO / 25.8 VIRGO /
    16.9 LIBRA
1972 CANCER / 8.9 LEO
1973 LIBRA / 14.9 SCORPIO
1974 LEO / 8.9 VIRGO
1975 CANCER / 3.9 LEO
1976 VIRGO / 2.9 LIBRA
1977 CANCER / 29.8 LEO
1978 LIBRA / 8.9 SCORPIO
1979 VIRGO / 16.9 LIBRA
1980 CANCER / 8.9 LEO
1981 LIBRA / 14.9 SCORPIO
1982 LEO / 7.9 VIRGO
1983 VIRGO / 28.8 LEO
1984 VIRGO / 2.9 LIBRA
1985 CANCER / 28.8 LEO
1986 LIBRA / 8.9 SCORPIO
1987 VIRGO / 15.9 LIBRA
1988 CANCER / 7.9 LEO
1989 LIBRA / 13.9 SCORPIO
1990 LEO / 7.9 VIRGO
1991 LEO
1992 VIRGO / 1.9 LIBRA
1993 CANCER / 28.8 LEO
1994 LIBRA / 8.9 SCORPIO
1995 VIRGO / 15.9 LIBRA
1996 CANCER / 7.9 LEO
1997 LIBRA / 12.9 SCORPIO
1998 LEO / 6.9 VIRGO
1999 LEO
2000 VIRGO / 1.9 LIBRA
2001 CANCER / 28.8 LEO
2002 LIBRA / 8.9 SCORPIO
2003 VIRGO / 15.9 LIBRA
2004 CANCER / 6.9 LEO
2005 LIBRA / 10.9 SCORPIO
2006 LEO / 4.9 VIRGO
2007 LEO
2008 VIRGO / 1.9 LIBRA
2009 CANCER / 28.8 LEO
2010 LIBRA / 8.9 SCORPIO
2011 VIRGO / 15.9 LIBRA
2012 CANCER / 6.9 LEO
2013 LIBRA / 10.9 SCORPIO
2014 LEO / 4.9 VIRGO
2015 LEO
2016 VIRGO / 31.8 LIBRA

VENUS THROUGH THE ZODIAC SIGNS

Venus in Aries

Amongst other things, the position of Venus in Aries indicates a fondness for travel, music and all creative pursuits. Your nature tends to be affectionate and you try not to create confusion or difficulty for others if it can be avoided. Many people with this planetary position have a great love of the theatre, and mental stimulation is of the greatest importance. Early romantic attachments are common with Venus in Aries, so it is very important to establish a genuine sense of romantic continuity. Early marriage is not recommended, especially if it is based on sympathy. You may give your heart a little too readily on occasions.

Venus in Taurus

You are capable of very deep feelings and your emotions tend to last for a very long time. This makes you a trusting partner and lover, whose constancy is second to none. In life you are precise and careful and always try to do things the right way. Although this means an ordered life, which you are comfortable with, it can also lead you to be rather too fussy for your own good. Despite your pleasant nature, you are very fixed in your opinions and quite able to speak your mind. Others are attracted to you and historical astrologers always quoted this position of Venus as being very fortunate in terms of marriage. However, if you find yourself involved in a failed relationship, it could take you a long time to trust again.

Venus in Gemini

As with all associations related to Gemini, you tend to be quite versatile, anxious for change and intelligent in your dealings with the world at large. You may gain money from more than one source but you are equally good at spending it. There is an inference here that you are a good communicator, either in the written or the spoken word, and you love to be in the company of interesting people. Always on the look-out for culture, you may also be very fond of music, and love to indulge the curious and cultured side of your nature. In romance you tend to have more than one relationship and could find yourself associated with someone who has previously been a friend or even a distant relative.

Venus in Cancer

You often stay close to home because you are very fond of family and enjoy many of your most treasured moments when you are with those you love. Being naturally sympathetic, you will always do anything you can to support those around you, even people you hardly know at all. This charitable side of your nature is your most noticeable trait and is one of the reasons why others are naturally so fond of you. Being receptive and in some cases even psychic, you can see through to the soul of most of those with whom you come into contact. You may not commence too many romantic attachments but when you do give your heart, it tends to be unconditionally.

Venus in Leo

It must become quickly obvious to almost anyone you meet that you are kind, sympathetic and yet determined enough to stand up for anyone or anything that is truly important to you. Bright and sunny, you warm the world with your natural enthusiasm and would rarely do anything to hurt those around you, or at least not intentionally. In romance you are ardent and sincere, though some may find your style just a little overpowering. Gains come through your contacts with other people and this could be especially true with regard to romance, for love and money often come hand in hand for those who were born with Venus in Leo. People claim to understand you, though you are more complex than you seem.

Venus in Virgo

Your nature could well be fairly quiet no matter what your Sun sign might be, though this fact often manifests itself as an inner peace and does not prevent you from being basically sociable. Some delays and even the odd disappointment in love cannot be ruled out with this planetary position, though it's a fact that you will usually find the happiness you look for in the end. Catapulting yourself into romantic entanglements that you know to be rather ill-advised is not sensible, and it would be better to wait before you commit yourself exclusively to any one person. It is the essence of your nature to serve the world at large and through doing so it is possible that you will attract money at some stage in your life.

Venus in Libra

Venus is very comfortable in Libra and bestows upon those people who have this planetary position a particular sort of kindness that is easy to recognise. This is a very good position for all sorts of friendships and also for romantic attachments that usually bring much joy into your life. Few individuals with Venus in Libra would avoid marriage and since you are capable of great depths of love, it is likely that you will find a contented personal life. You like to mix with people of integrity and intelligence but don't take kindly to scruffy surroundings or work that means getting your hands too dirty. Careful speculation, good business dealings and money through marriage all seem fairly likely.

Venus in Scorpio

You are quite open and tend to spend money quite freely, even on those occasions when you don't have very much. Although your intentions are always good, there are times when you get yourself in to the odd scrape and this can be particularly true when it comes to romance, which you may come to late or from a rather unexpected direction. Certainly you have the power to be happy and to make others contented on the way, but you will find the odd stumbling block on your journey through life and it could seem that you have to work harder than those around you. As a result of this, you gain a much deeper understanding of the true value of personal happiness than many people ever do, and are likely to achieve true contentment in the end.

Venus in Sagittarius

You are lighthearted, cheerful and always able to see the funny side of any situation. These facts enhance your popularity. You should never have to look too far to find romantic interest in your life, though it is just possible that you might be too willing to commit yourself before you are certain that someone is right for you. Part of the problem here extends to other areas of life too. The fact is that you like variety in everything and so can tire of situations that fail to offer it. All the same, if you choose wisely and learn to understand your restless side, then great happiness can be yours.

Venus in Capricorn

The most notable trait that comes from Venus in this position is that it makes you trustworthy and able to take on all sorts of responsibilities in life. People are instinctively fond of you and love you all the more because you are always ready to help those who are in any form of need. Social and business popularity can be yours and there is a magnetic quality to your nature that is particularly attractive in a romantic sense. Anyone who wants a partner for a lover, a spouse and a good friend too would almost certainly look in your direction. Constancy is the hallmark of your nature and unfaithfulness would goes against the grain. You might sometimes be a little too trusting.

Venus in Aquarius

This location of Venus offers a fondness for travel and a desire to try out something new at every possible opportunity. You are extremely easy to get along with and tend to have many friends from varied backgrounds, classes and inclinations. You like to live a distinct sort of life and gain a great deal from moving about, both in a career sense and with regard to your home. It is not out of the question that you could form a romantic attachment to someone who comes from far away or be attracted to a person of a distinctly artistic and original nature. What you cannot stand is jealousy, for you have friends of both sexes and would want to keep things that way.

Venus in Pisces

The first thing people tend to notice about you is your wonderful, warm smile. Being very charitable by nature you will do anything to help others, even if you don't know them well. Much of your life may be spent sorting out situations for other people, but it is very important to feel that you are living for yourself too. In the main, you remain cheerful, and tend to be quite attractive to other people. Where romantic attachments are concerned, you could be drawn to people who are significantly older or younger than yourself or to someone with a unique career or point of view. It might be best for you to avoid marrying whilst you are still very young.

VIRGO:
2015 DIARY PAGES

October
2015

1 THURSDAY ☿ *Moon Age Day 18 Moon Sign Taurus*

There are some wonderful surprises in store for Virgo today, but you will have to keep your eye on the ball to gain from any of them. Not everyone is on your side at work, but those who aren't probably have something to gain from opposing you. Focus on your own circumstances and don't rise to the bait!

2 FRIDAY ☿ *Moon Age Day 19 Moon Sign Gemini*

A time of social highlights comes along, with plenty of opportunities to have fun. Present astrological trends could lead you to cast your mind forward to the medium-term future, perhaps even Christmas. Longer term plans might have to be put on hold for a variety of different and generally tedious reasons.

3 SATURDAY ☿ *Moon Age Day 20 Moon Sign Gemini*

You definitely enjoy being busy today and can make the best out of almost any sort of situation. Watch out for the odd minor mishap, probably brought about as a result of carelessness exhibited by someone else. Your present quick thinking makes you good to have around in any tight corner.

4 SUNDAY ☿ *Moon Age Day 21 Moon Sign Gemini*

Romance not only becomes more likely, but potentially more rewarding, too. Things that irritated you earlier in the week are now much more likely to make you laugh instead. It might be good to look for a change of scene and an alteration in your routines this Sunday. Money matters may also begin to look stronger.

5 MONDAY ☿ *Moon Age Day 22 Moon Sign Cancer*

Now is the time to be enjoying good social trends and letting people know just how capable you are. Controlling all aspects of your life isn't going to be particularly easy, but you care less about certain issues at this time. Relationships should be working out particularly well and offering new insights.

6 TUESDAY ☿ *Moon Age Day 23 Moon Sign Cancer*

There are warnings of a rather more problematic series of trends for today, some of which could find you disagreeing with people who normally are no problem. The fault could be yours, so it is important to stand back and look again. As long as you are reasonable, any sort of compromise eventually becomes possible.

7 WEDNESDAY ☿ *Moon Age Day 24 Moon Sign Leo*

Professional developments should be working out quite well, leaving you with more time to please yourself. If life is plain sailing, take some time out. The year is growing older and there are still some personal incentives you have not looked at specifically. A big plan is worth another, very careful look now.

8 THURSDAY ☿ *Moon Age Day 25 Moon Sign Leo*

It is likely you could talk anyone into doing anything for you now. There are one or two individuals around at present whom you look at with slight mistrust, though probably for no good reason. There won't be time to do everything you would wish today, so it is important to look carefully at priorities.

9 FRIDAY ☿ *Moon Age Day 26 Moon Sign Virgo*

The Moon moves gradually into your zodiac sign today, and brings with it a desire to do as much as you can, as quickly as proves to be possible. Despite a wealth of opportunities it would advisable to tackle jobs one at a time. At least that way you can be sure you do all of them to the best of your ability.

10 SATURDAY ☿ *Moon Age Day 27 Moon Sign Virgo*

The Moon is still on your side, so get cracking and keep busy. With everything to prove and a vitality that is second to none, it's unlikely that you will be overlooked in anything. Routines are really for the birds at this time and you tend to do whatever takes your fancy, at the time that seems most providential.

11 SUNDAY ☿ *Moon Age Day 28 Moon Sign Virgo*

Talks with others can find you making a sort of headway you hadn't been expecting. For many of you, this is a day of rest, but you've been there and done that earlier this week. As a result, don't be surprised to find yourself out of bed early and anxious to get on with life just as quickly as you are able.

12 MONDAY *Moon Age Day 29 Moon Sign Libra*

There are signs that this could prove to be one of the better days of the month for your romantic life. There are overtures likely to come from both expected and unexpected directions and a wealth of interest from friends, too. If everyone seems to be talking about you, that's because you are so interesting now.

13 TUESDAY *Moon Age Day 0 Moon Sign Libra*

Much of the day is geared towards practical matters, though it doesn't have to be that way. Virtually nothing in your life would fall apart if you decided to take some time off. There are people around who long for your company and a host of activities that are going the way you would wish. Enjoy yourself for a while.

14 WEDNESDAY *Moon Age Day 1 Moon Sign Scorpio*

Right now, making up your mind regarding even a crucial personal matter is not going to be at all easy. It might be best to defer decisions until later. By that time you will have had the chance to seek out the advice of someone you trust implicitly. Friends are easy to make at this time, and are not likely to be lost later.

15 THURSDAY   *Moon Age Day 2 Moon Sign Scorpio*

The practical world is still doing you the odd favour, allowing you to make gains, particularly in a financial sense. Rules and regulations are not too difficult to follow now and you find yourself well able to conform when it is necessary. Help a friend with a specific problem and also be supportive of family members.

16 FRIDAY   *Moon Age Day 3 Moon Sign Scorpio*

This is a time during which love life and relationships should be putting a very definite smile on your face. If you don't have the time to do everything you wish in a practical sense, be willing to leave some of it for another day. Most of the people you meet today prove to be very reasonable.

17 SATURDAY   *Moon Age Day 4 Moon Sign Sagittarius*

You are at your very best now in small gatherings, and especially so when mixing with people you already know. The slightly shy side of Virgo is showing and you also demonstrate a reserve that casual acquaintances might not understand. Nevertheless, in a professional sense, you still display confidence.

18 SUNDAY   *Moon Age Day 5 Moon Sign Sagittarius*

You may discover that some people are far less assertive than usual, and you can put that down to your own attitude. It is a fact that you don't brook any interference right now and that those around you realise the fact. The more you get done early today, the greater is the likelihood that you can enjoy a peaceful Sunday later.

19 MONDAY   *Moon Age Day 6 Moon Sign Capricorn*

Only you can decide whether to believe everything you hear today, but there could be some fibbers around. Mostly, these will represent people who are charming and quite incapable of doing you any harm, but you need to be on your guard all the same. Keep an eye on your health.

20 TUESDAY *Moon Age Day 7 Moon Sign Capricorn*

Today could be a mixed bag, but is still likely to favour you in a general sense. If there are any frustrations, these are likely to come about as a result of the attitude of colleagues, some of whom are ploughing a very different furrow from your own. Keep abreast of things that are happening in your immediate locality.

21 WEDNESDAY *Moon Age Day 8 Moon Sign Capricorn*

Work and practical affairs keep you generally busy today and offer you the comfort of knowing that life is running in a smooth and steady way. There probably won't be too much in the way of excitement, though you are hardly likely to be worried by that fact at the moment.

22 THURSDAY *Moon Age Day 9 Moon Sign Aquarius*

You may discover that in financial matters you have to take a very patient point of view, which could make it difficult to be immediate in your approach. This can lead to some inner conflict because you really do want to get ahead today. Creative potential remains essentially high, with some wonderful ideas coming along.

23 FRIDAY *Moon Age Day 10 Moon Sign Aquarius*

Although you are feeling quite assertive today, you do need to watch your step in some ways. Not everyone is working towards your ultimate good, no matter what they say to the contrary. Problems are not likely to arise with relatives or friends, though colleagues could be more of a problem.

24 SATURDAY *Moon Age Day 11 Moon Sign Pisces*

A two-day lunar low is at hand. Normally this might be a cause for some concern, but you have been pushing yourself so hard of late, a reduction in pressure ought to be no bad thing. Comfort and security are on your mind now and you might even decide to take a day more or less completely to yourself.

25 SUNDAY

Moon Age Day 12 Moon Sign Pisces

When things get quiet, Virgo subjects can spend time pampering themselves. Why not? You have put in a great deal of effort so far this month and you deserve to have a decent rest. On the other hand, if you have to work today do as little as you can and allow others to fill in where possible. This could be a fairly uneventful day.

26 MONDAY

Moon Age Day 13 Moon Sign Aries

Today should be reasonably fulfilling in a workaday sense, though better still in terms of your social and personal life. Romance seems to rear its head on a number of occasions, and particularly so if you put yourself out. This might be a good time to buy someone a bunch of flowers or some other small gift.

27 TUESDAY

Moon Age Day 14 Moon Sign Aries

You need to get on with something simple and relatively free from stress if it proves to be at all possible right now. You don't have too much energy in reserve, which is why you are willing to let others do things that you would normally wish to deal with yourself. When they do, avoid being critical of their methods.

28 WEDNESDAY

Moon Age Day 15 Moon Sign Taurus

Right now you have the knack of getting your point of view across in a very positive way and can really get on famously when in the company of people whose attitude stimulates you in any way. Frank, free and quite outspoken, you can definitely make today your own with only a little effort.

29 THURSDAY

Moon Age Day 16 Moon Sign Taurus

Present relationships tend to be quite harmonious, even with people you don't always trust too much. Those folk you have seen as competitors now want to help you out, that is, if you are not too suspicious to take their help on board. You seem to be quite intuitive at present and can easily make up your mind about anything.

30 FRIDAY

Moon Age Day 17 Moon Sign Gemini

Your acquisitive tendencies are strong now, which isn't so strange for the zodiac sign of Virgo. You know what you want from life, and have a pretty good idea about how you intend to get it. Some would call you calculating, but since you bear the good of others in mind, this isn't really the case.

31 SATURDAY

Moon Age Day 18 Moon Sign Gemini

Good times in relationships mark the weekend out as feeling safe, warm and generally comfortable. Although you can't count on the support of everyone you know, in the main the people you rely on the most come up trumps on your behalf. Concentrate on issues that can make you better off financially.

November

2015

1 SUNDAY

Moon Age Day 19 Moon Sign Cancer

The pursuit of wealth might now be on your list of priorities. Virgo may not be the most acquisitive of the zodiac signs, but it isn't too far behind. It's all down to a sense of security, which Virgo desires. Casting your mind forward in time, you can now do some deals that will feather your nest in years to come.

2 MONDAY

Moon Age Day 20 Moon Sign Cancer

Stay clear of disagreements today if you possibly can. It would be better not to interact too much with people at all, rather than to find yourself involved in pointless rows. Such a state of affairs is far less likely in terms of deep attachments. Virgo subjects who are looking for love should have some success now.

3 TUESDAY

Moon Age Day 21 Moon Sign Leo

The period during which help is at hand if you need it continues apace, so don't assume you have do everything for yourself now. On the contrary, people are only too willing to put themselves out on your behalf and will continue to do so for a while. Even those you don't know very well can be considerate.

4 WEDNESDAY

Moon Age Day 22 Moon Sign Leo

The most powerful focus today is upon close, personal attachments, but that doesn't mean you are ignoring the world at large. On the contrary, you virtually demand to be out there in the middle of whatever is happening. You might not see all that much of family members today because you are likely to be so busy.

5 THURSDAY
Moon Age Day 23 Moon Sign Leo

There isn't a great deal of dynamic ambition today, but this is only a very short trend and due to end almost immediately. For the moment, you will be happy to watch life go by and less inclined than of late to look for riotous social company. Part of your nature is actually very nostalgic around now.

6 FRIDAY
Moon Age Day 24 Moon Sign Virgo

Get an early start today and acknowledge right from the start that fortune now favours the brave. The lunar high brings you the chance to shine and should lift your spirits considerably, bearing in mind the way you have been thinking and acting across the last few days. Be prepared to take the odd chance.

7 SATURDAY
Moon Age Day 25 Moon Sign Virgo

Another potentially good day and a time during which you will be making the most of just about any opportunity that comes your way. Creatively speaking, you know what looks and feels right and you can gain support from some unexpected directions. You could surprise yourself with your boldness right now.

8 SUNDAY
Moon Age Day 26 Moon Sign Libra

A change of scene would suit you down to the ground, even though the necessities of life could make that somewhat difficult to achieve. You should remain fairly busy and be concentrating on making things better for yourself in a financial sense especially. Family demands are present, though easy to deal with.

9 MONDAY
Moon Age Day 27 Moon Sign Libra

When tasks have to be completed today, you are inclined to want to do everything your own way. That's fine, just as long as you can persuade others that you know what you are talking about. There will be some awkward types around at the moment, so you could have to work quite hard to get the message across.

10 TUESDAY
Moon Age Day 28 Moon Sign Libra

You might feel that you are less in control of your own life in some ways, but this should not really prove to be a particular issue as long as you are willing to co-operate with others. Get on your side those who have ideas that broadly parallel your own, and don't be afraid to take a few calculated risks.

11 WEDNESDAY
Moon Age Day 29 Moon Sign Scorpio

Someone might be trying to put you down in the estimation of others, or at least that's how it will appear to you right now. It is likely that you are not looking at things quite as logically as would normally be the case and emotions can get in the way. Most important is to keep a smile on your face, even when you feel jumpy.

12 THURSDAY
Moon Age Day 0 Moon Sign Scorpio

This is not a day during which you can afford to take anything for granted. You should check and double-check all details, especially if any of them are related to travel. Staying in one place could prove to be something of a bind, particularly when movement looks so potentially interesting and rewarding.

13 FRIDAY
Moon Age Day 1 Moon Sign Sagittarius

Your love life is apt to be a high point today. Single Virgo subjects ought to find a good deal of attention coming their way, whilst those involved in settled relationships can achieve an even better understanding and contentment. Practical progress could be slightly restricted, but since you are busy in other ways, it won't matter.

14 SATURDAY
Moon Age Day 2 Moon Sign Sagittarius

You can probably expect a good deal more attention coming your way around this time. This will happen in both a personal and in a more general sense. Popularity is everything to you now and you won't hold back in terms of the love you offer in return. Almost anyone can feel your warmth now.

15 SUNDAY *Moon Age Day 3 Moon Sign Sagittarius*

A more settled period comes along as far as your personal life is concerned. Don't be too quick to offer advice, because you could find yourself refusing the same suggestions yourself before very long. Courage is necessary in public situations but you should come good in sporting activities.

16 MONDAY *Moon Age Day 4 Moon Sign Capricorn*

Minor disruptions to domestic peace and harmony typify the sort of trends that stand around you right now. Try not to get more involved in them than is strictly necessary and definitely stay away from other people's rows. You need peace and quiet, though whether you can find it today remains to be seen.

17 TUESDAY *Moon Age Day 5 Moon Sign Capricorn*

It's a time for getting down to the real nitty-gritty of issues. Don't be sidetracked and make certain that you know others are telling the truth. How can you be certain? Well, at the moment your intuition is turned up high, so few people will be able to fool you.

18 WEDNESDAY *Moon Age Day 6 Moon Sign Aquarius*

Things could be slightly sluggish in a professional sense, so it would be best to only do what you have to at work. Domestically speaking, life should be rather easier to address and in truth, you will be happiest today when at home. You might relish the prospect of simply putting your feet up.

19 THURSDAY *Moon Age Day 7 Moon Sign Aquarius*

Friends could turn out to be quite helpful, often in fairly unexpected ways. Don't be too proud to accept assistance if it's offered, even though in at least some cases you could manage better on your own. Keep a sense of proportion when dealing with issues that have stumped you in the past. Persistence pays off in the end.

20 FRIDAY
Moon Age Day 8 Moon Sign Pisces

You could find yourself receiving support, rather than offering it. Potentially speaking, the arrival of the lunar low can take the wind out of your sails, but if you are prepared, the situation will not be half so bad. There are confidences to keep, and although practical matters are on the back burner, love and attention are very noticeable.

21 SATURDAY
Moon Age Day 9 Moon Sign Pisces

Compromise is your middle name today, or at least it if isn't, then it should be. You can get more today by being willing to give a little than at just about any other time this month. Some nostalgia creeps in, but that is part of the way the lunar low makes its presence felt in your life. By tomorrow you will be flying high again.

22 SUNDAY
Moon Age Day 10 Moon Sign Aries

You will have to fall back on your own wits today, because people are not all that reliable. The problem is that you have very exacting standards at present and won't be too keen to relinquish control in any case. Be prepared to alter your ideas when circumstances don't turn out as you may have expected.

23 MONDAY
Moon Age Day 11 Moon Sign Aries

You should feel good about yourself and life in general as the week gets started. There is tremendous scope for advancement at work, plus extra incentive to go out and get what you want. Although you will come across obstacles at some stage during the day, these are unlikely to hold you back.

24 TUESDAY
Moon Age Day 12 Moon Sign Taurus

A generally lucrative period continues, though you won't have everything you would wish today. Part of the reason for this is that some of your expectations are not entirely realistic. This will lead to disappointments if you fail to realise how life really is. A more contemplative phase is needed.

25 WEDNESDAY   *Moon Age Day 13 Moon Sign Taurus*

Your mind works swiftly, leading you to arrive at some quite staggering conclusions and often on the spur of the moment. The middle of the working week makes specific demands of you, and especially so at work. You may be quite pleased to lay down some responsibilities by the evening.

26 THURSDAY   *Moon Age Day 14 Moon Sign Gemini*

There is little time for intimate concerns today, because material and practical considerations are taking up so much of your time. All things considered, this would be an ideal time to take a day off, though the way your mind is working at the moment this is less than likely.

27 FRIDAY   *Moon Age Day 15 Moon Sign Gemini*

Work-wise, someone may be putting you in the picture regarding an issue that has been at the forefront of your mind of late. Getting to know what is going on in your vicinity seems especially important now, which is why you are listening so carefully to everything that is being said.

28 SATURDAY   *Moon Age Day 16 Moon Sign Cancer*

A thoughtful approach to specific matters is necessary early in the day, but by the afternoon you should be feeling quite active again. You respond very well to the overtures of your partner and will be quite happy to get out of the house. Perhaps a shopping trip is on the cards.

29 SUNDAY   *Moon Age Day 17 Moon Sign Cancer*

You have little real patience with specific emotional matters today and you may consider that someone you know well is acting in a fairly irrational manner. There are some unusual people about whose ideas and actions could fascinate you somewhat, but don't be drawn into anything weird.

30 MONDAY
Moon Age Day 18 Moon Sign Cancer

Personal concerns or wishes can be successfully addressed today, perhaps partly as a result of information that comes through the post or over the internet. Concern for your friends is also apparent, as you try to help someone sort out a thorny problem associated with relationships.

December

2015

1 TUESDAY
Moon Age Day 19 Moon Sign Leo

You are well aware what elements of your life deserve your attention today, even though one or two people might think that they know different. Spend time with family members and do what you can to support a friend who could well be going through a rough period right now.

2 WEDNESDAY
Moon Age Day 20 Moon Sign Leo

Compromises in relationships are a natural part of what you will encounter at the present time. If you refuse to make them, problems could come along later. Stay away from rows in your family or indeed amongst friends. The problem is not one of failing to hold your own, but rather of being too aggressive.

3 THURSDAY
Moon Age Day 21 Moon Sign Virgo

The start of the month sees you reaching your mental and physical peak. It doesn't matter what you take on today, you have the energy and determination to see it through properly. Gains can be made as a result of meetings and discussions that could have taken place some time ago.

4 FRIDAY
Moon Age Day 22 Moon Sign Virgo

This is still very much a go-ahead period and offers you the vitality to get everything you need to be done out of the way before the weekend. You ought to be in fine spirits and more than willing to have a go at more or less anything. Stay away from contentious topics in conversation.

5 SATURDAY
Moon Age Day 23 Moon Sign Libra

Some of your efforts at keeping life under control are going wrong. The results are likely to be more amusing than annoying, though there could be times today when the odd frustration will creep in. Once again, it is important to avoid confrontation with people who are not really worth your effort.

6 SUNDAY
Moon Age Day 24 Moon Sign Libra

Although there is little in the way of harmony in your relationships today, part of the reason could be frustrations you find difficult to address. Talk to people and truly listen to what they have to say. Compromise is necessary and that isn't a particularly tall order for you at the moment.

7 MONDAY
Moon Age Day 25 Moon Sign Libra

Though career aims might have rather less going for them than has been the case lately, you should certainly be enjoying yourself in terms of your personal life. Compliments are easy to come by and you are likely to turn heads wherever you go, especially by the evening.

8 TUESDAY
Moon Age Day 26 Moon Sign Scorpio

Financially speaking, there could be some minor improvements now – and not a moment too soon, with Christmas so close. Nevertheless, you need to spend wisely and to look out for those bargains that lie around every corner. All in all, this could be one of the best days of December for shopping.

9 WEDNESDAY
Moon Age Day 27 Moon Sign Scorpio

Personal and intimate matters are the most rewarding of all this Wednesday. You will be quite busy moment by moment, but you need to save time to show your lover how much you care. The response you get is very positive and should see you finishing the day on a high note.

10 THURSDAY *Moon Age Day 28 Moon Sign Sagittarius*

You could easily get the feeling that you are speaking out of turn today. That's fine, but unless you say what you think, how on earth will others know? It's really a case of speaking the truth to shame the devil, just as long as you remember to use a little Mercurial tact on the way.

11 FRIDAY *Moon Age Day 0 Moon Sign Sagittarius*

The time is right to establish good relations with just about anyone, even people who have not been your favourites in the past. There is a good chance that you are being taken more seriously now and that you might make a friend of someone who was never very kind to you in years gone by.

12 SATURDAY *Moon Age Day 1 Moon Sign Sagittarius*

Although today starts out fairly steady, things could soon hot up. Progress is hard to see at first, which is why by lunchtime you'll have to put in that extra bit of effort that can make all the difference. By the evening, you can be the life and soul of any party. If there isn't one on offer, you might create a shindig yourself.

13 SUNDAY *Moon Age Day 2 Moon Sign Capricorn*

You might have a sense today that you can't rely on anyone except yourself. Up to a point that might be the case, but you ought to give friends the benefit of the doubt all the same. Offer others a helping hand in specific tasks that are familiar to you, but don't get in the way if younger people are seeking independence.

14 MONDAY *Moon Age Day 3 Moon Sign Capricorn*

You could be in quite a hurry to complete a particular project and will be quite anxious not to allow anything to get in your way. In all probability this is something you should have done days or weeks ago, but right now is hardly the right time to address it. Put it on the shelf until the New Year.

15 TUESDAY
Moon Age Day 4 Moon Sign Aquarius

Beware a heavy-handed approach at home, particularly with younger people, who are only seeking to spread their wings. You should learn to trust, as others are willing to trust you. Only rarely are you likely to be let down. Confidence to do the right thing is there, but you need to look for it.

16 WEDNESDAY
Moon Age Day 5 Moon Sign Aquarius

Your social instincts are very definitely engaged today and you can be the best company imaginable. This is far from being a normal sort of Wednesday as far as you are concerned, even if you have to work. When you are not toiling, there are gains to be made through love and new friendship.

17 THURSDAY
Moon Age Day 6 Moon Sign Pisces

Get ready for a couple of days during which it will be difficult to get everything you want from life. The lunar low is holding you back, but not all that much. As long as you stick to planning, and leave a few of the more concrete jobs until the very end of the week, you will hardly be held up at all this month.

18 FRIDAY
Moon Age Day 7 Moon Sign Pisces

Stick to the simple things of life and spend some time spoiling yourself. There is an active and very demanding period ahead, so it won't do you any harm to charge up those batteries. Confidence isn't really dented, unless you come face to face with people who seem determined to put you down.

19 SATURDAY
Moon Age Day 8 Moon Sign Aries

Get ready to make tracks and get ahead professionally. With one eye on Christmas and the other on what you want to achieve materially, there isn't a great deal of time to spare right now. Don't overbook yourself for the weekend. It's the last one before Christmas and there might be shopping you have forgotten.

20 SUNDAY
Moon Age Day 9 Moon Sign Aries

Getting along with others isn't too difficult this weekend, just as long as they are willing to do exactly what you ask. There is a danger that you are being rather more selfish than usual. Get out and about, if you can, though it is likely that your main destination will be the local shopping centre.

21 MONDAY
Moon Age Day 10 Moon Sign Aries

Communication issues are to the fore today and you need to make sure that you get any message across intact. Don't be too quick to judge others for merely doing things you have done yourself in the past. It would be sensible to take a sympathetic point of view when possible today.

22 TUESDAY
Moon Age Day 11 Moon Sign Taurus

Yet again, the circumstances surrounding your home life and domestic issues generally seem to be going your way. There is a great sense of comfort and security about now, mixed with a tinge of nostalgia, probably on account of the time of year. Despite this, you must be realistic.

23 WEDNESDAY
Moon Age Day 12 Moon Sign Taurus

You now seem to be in such a hurry to get things done, you are forgetting some of the most important details. If you want to avoid having to stop and then begin all over again, you need to concentrate. Friends are there to lend a helping hand, if you give them the chance.

24 THURSDAY
Moon Age Day 13 Moon Sign Gemini

There are almost certainly some surprises on the social scene, together with a desire to get on well with people generally. Because you are a Virgo, it is likely that you have everything prepared. Don't be at all surprised if nostalgic associations take over at some stage during the day, particularly if you have children.

25 FRIDAY
Moon Age Day 14 Moon Sign Gemini

A lovely mix of planetary trends surrounds you during Christmas Day. Some of them are quiet, so you may not choose to be socially active all the time. You receive significant emotional support and return it in kind. Not surprisingly, family associations are well accented right now.

26 SATURDAY
Moon Age Day 15 Moon Sign Cancer

It is the home-based side of Christmas that appeals to you the most this time around, though you are chatty, carefree and very good company in any situation. There could be presents of a very singular nature coming your way, one or two of them from a most unexpected direction.

27 SUNDAY
Moon Age Day 16 Moon Sign Cancer

Love affairs are well highlighted today, as is travel. Perhaps you will see people you haven't shared an hour or two with for quite a long time. Although you might be bullied into doing things that go against the grain, you could be quite surprised in the end. It is worth putting yourself out.

28 MONDAY
Moon Age Day 17 Moon Sign Leo

Whatever you decide to take on board today, bear in mind that energies are limited and that your recovery rate is not what it might normally be. Because of this, you need to restrict your activities just a little, whilst at the same time making yourself fully conversant with what is happening around you.

29 TUESDAY
Moon Age Day 18 Moon Sign Leo

Don't be surprised if the general pace of events tends to slow significantly around this time. There are quieter astrological trends predominating today, not the least of which is supplied by the Moon. Being where it is at present, it turns your attention specifically in the direction of home and family.

30 WEDNESDAY   *Moon Age Day 19 Moon Sign Virgo*

You may be in for the best and most protracted New Year bash you have known for years. Today and tomorrow coincide with the lunar high, offering a fun-filled attitude, together with an instinctive knowledge regarding how to keep other people laughing. Almost anything you do today is tinged with genius.

31 THURSDAY   *Moon Age Day 20 Moon Sign Virgo*

It appears that this is a particularly good phase for any sort of intimacy between yourself and your partner. For those who are not attached, it might be that a friendship takes on a different sort of meaning in your life. Resolutions made today are likely to be as a result of a great deal of thought earlier in the year.

VIRGO:
2016 DIARY PAGES

VIRGO:
YOUR YEAR IN BRIEF

The accent is definitely on success for Virgo this year, even if you may encounter a few slight distractions on the way. Starting very positively, January and February mark a great start to the year and offer new incentives at work. Despite the winter weather you are progressive, anxious to travel and happy to do whatever is necessary to get ahead. People from the past emerge into your life again and may bring with them a few significant memories.

With the arrival of the spring, March and April will see you in a fairly jolly frame of mind and you will be every bit the social animal that Virgo can be when working at its best. Not everything is going to go your way and some extra care will be necessary with finances, but March in particular has much to offer in a personal sense and also brings you the chance to get ahead at work. April could bring all manner of surprising new ideas which should have a bearing on your family and personal life.

Summer brings Virgo to a whole series of new realisations and May, in particular, is likely to be an eventful and meaningful month. Look out for new business opportunities and greater bargaining power. Meanwhile, June looks particularly good from a personal point of view with either the start of a new relationship or the deepening of existing ties. June should also be good for travel.

By July you will be enjoying what the summer has to offer and it is at this time that your absolute desire to spread your wings and fly becomes most obvious. Both long and short journeys will be possible, both for business and pleasure. Make this a time to open a new dialogue with people who might have been difficult to deal with in the past and also plan well where your finances are concerned. August continues the favourable trends but could find you facing slight personal frustrations.

September brings additional opportunities for travel, which for some will mean long-distance journeys that offer financial as well as personal gains. New ideas come along all the time and during October you will have the chance to put some of these to the test, whilst at the same time gaining powerful new allies. Routines are cast aside this autumn as you are in a vibrant and go-getting mood.

November and December are likely to be stimulating and will bring new interests into your life. Virgo is very active and generally competitive at this time. Christmas is likely to prove happy but beware of some small problems throughout the festive season which you may need to address quickly. By the New Year you will be happy to join in the party atmosphere and will be looking ahead positively.

January 2016

1 FRIDAY
Moon Age Day 21   Moon Sign Virgo

What a way to start a year, with the Moon in your zodiac sign. This means you will be up and smiling early in the day, even if you do have a hangover! Keep a sense of proportion about what you can manage to get done but start to put all those New Year plans into action as soon as possible.

2 SATURDAY
Moon Age Day 22   Moon Sign Libra

However long a particular task takes is the time you have to spend on it. That is self-evident to you, but may not be to other people. There is a deep and profound spirituality about your thinking at the moment, which is probably why others are seeking you out for help and advice.

3 SUNDAY
Moon Age Day 23   Moon Sign Libra

It may appear that this is a good time to sit and think about the good old days. Nostalgia is fine and has its place in our emotional suitcase but it probably doesn't help you too much as a rule, and certainly not now. Try to look forward and enjoy the positive prospects you find around yourself at this time.

4 MONDAY
Moon Age Day 24   Moon Sign Scorpio

A professional matter now proves to be very uplifting as you discover the right way to go about a particular task that might have been something of a mystery to you before. Concentration becomes easier and you settle down to accepting that this is a new year and that life could prove to be somewhat different now.

5 TUESDAY　　　　*Moon Age Day 25　Moon Sign Scorpio*

You may not find it easy to bend career situations the way you would wish right now and so it might be best not to try. Concentrating on the matter at hand won't be easy and you should be aware of the broader picture of life in any case. Something or someone very unusual may come into your life soon.

6 WEDNESDAY　☿　*Moon Age Day 26　Moon Sign Scorpio*

Issues in the practical world ought to be going more your way now, though you should pay particular attention to little details, something that Virgo is naturally inclined to do anyway. You can probably get a great deal more done than you actually expect, particularly if you take some proffered help.

7 THURSDAY　☿　*Moon Age Day 27　Moon Sign Sagittarius*

'The more the merrier' is the adage today, both in terms of the jobs you are taking on and with regard to the number of people you are entertaining in your life. It doesn't matter whether you know people well or not. Your communication skills are good and you are able to come to terms with a few past errors.

8 FRIDAY　☿　*Moon Age Day 28　Moon Sign Sagittarius*

It could be said that getting what you want from life today is more important than almost anything else. Unfortunately, this makes you sound quite selfish, which isn't the case at all. On the contrary, most of what you want involves a better life for others, even if you do feather your own nest on the way.

9 SATURDAY　☿　*Moon Age Day 0　Moon Sign Capricorn*

Get out and about as much as you can today. It does you good to mix and mingle with others, despite the winter weather. In any case a change is as good as a rest, particularly if that means you are coming together with the sort of people who find you very attractive. Concentrate on money matters later today.

10 SUNDAY ☿ *Moon Age Day 1 Moon Sign Capricorn*

The simpler side of life is what seems to appeal to you most on this Sunday. Although the weather probably isn't too good and the days are short, you might benefit from some time spent in the fresh air. A healthier sort of Virgo who enjoys the outdoors now begins to emerge.

11 MONDAY ☿ *Moon Age Day 2 Moon Sign Aquarius*

You may suffer some losses in your professional life now, though these come along so that you can make gains later. That means being forward-looking and patient, two qualities you are not short of. Congratulations may be in order somewhere in the family and you should be happy to hand them out when the time comes.

12 TUESDAY ☿ *Moon Age Day 3 Moon Sign Aquarius*

This might be seen by others as a fairly self-indulgent time for Virgo. It's a facet of your nature that does crop up time and again, which is why Virgo people sometimes have to watch what they eat. There is no real tendency towards selfishness but you can sometimes be short of confidence. Don't turn to the Mars bars!

13 WEDNESDAY ☿ *Moon Age Day 4 Moon Sign Pisces*

It seems to be time to slow down and to take a break. You might be feeling somewhat lacking in sparkle and can really blame the position of the Moon for this. However, lunar lows are not usually too much of a problem to Virgo, which has a strong tendency to retreat into itself on occasion in any case.

14 THURSDAY ☿ *Moon Age Day 5 Moon Sign Pisces*

The position of the Moon could put a slight dampener on particular wishes you have for today. For example, there is no point at all in trying to move mountains. Things will come right when the time is right and your actions cannot change this. Simply enjoy sitting and watching the river of life today.

15 FRIDAY ☿ *Moon Age Day 6 Moon Sign Pisces*

Due to higher levels of physical energy today, it is clear that you are more willing to be out there at the front. Any form of sporting activity is well highlighted, and you wouldn't even mind being put on the spot in social situations at this time. Your creative potential tends to be very good.

16 SATURDAY ☿ *Moon Age Day 7 Moon Sign Aries*

A rather idealistic frame of mind might colour your judgements on this Saturday. It is true that the lunar low has passed, making you feel rather more energetic. However, you need to realise what is realistic in the short-term, and what can easily wait until a later date. Creative potential looks especially good at this time.

17 SUNDAY ☿ *Moon Age Day 8 Moon Sign Aries*

You probably want a little peace and quiet today, though finding it isn't likely to be easy. Later in the day you could learn something that is definitely to your advantage, but you will need to be careful not to give offence, particularly when all you are trying to do is to help.

18 MONDAY ☿ *Moon Age Day 9 Moon Sign Taurus*

Although it might sometimes appear that the progress you make is limited, nothing could be further from the truth. You have a very positive attitude, especially at work, and might be singled out for some significant attention from superiors. Extra responsibilities are not out of the question.

19 TUESDAY ☿ *Moon Age Day 10 Moon Sign Taurus*

There are times to argue, and periods when it is better to keep your counsel. The latter is the case right now, so avoid becoming involved in contentious issues. However, if you have no other choice than to express your opinions, you should do so with all the clarity and conviction presently in your arsenal.

20 WEDNESDAY ☿ *Moon Age Day 11   Moon Sign Gemini*

There are some strong supporting elements around now and you can make use of them. The fact is that one or two people think a great deal of you, and are willing to say so in public situations. Be willing to stand up for someone who is in trouble, even if you have to put yourself out significantly to do so.

21 THURSDAY ☿ *Moon Age Day 12   Moon Sign Gemini*

Good progress is possible, though can be somewhat restricted by a slightly negative attitude on your part if you are mixing with people who seem reluctant to give their all to situations. Be careful who you ally yourself with right now and, if possible, stick with those who have success stamped all over them.

22 FRIDAY ☿ *Moon Age Day 13   Moon Sign Cancer*

If there is one thing that is bound to get on your nerves at present, it is others telling you how you ought to live your life. Unfortunately, you don't have much option but to listen. Present trends prevent you from pushing ahead in a solo sense and you genuinely do need the support of those around you.

23 SATURDAY ☿ *Moon Age Day 14   Moon Sign Cancer*

The weekend brings you close to achieving a heart's desire, though maybe not in the way you would have expected. You are good at turning adversity into blessings and certainly know how to do so right now. Confidence remains essentially high, even if you express it in a low-key way.

24 SUNDAY ☿ *Moon Age Day 15   Moon Sign Leo*

You may lack the confidence to tackle unfamiliar projects, which is why it would be sensible for the moment to stick to some good old favourites. Creative potential is good, especially around the home, but you also need to have hobbies and pastimes of your own, which is something to think about now.

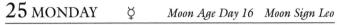

25 MONDAY ☿ *Moon Age Day 16   Moon Sign Leo*

A broad assessment of your life may now lead to certain changes. Don't be afraid to adopt an 'off with the old and on with the new' attitude, even if you find that this creates a good deal of upheaval. The year 2016 inevitably brings changes into your life in any case, so you may as well be in charge of them.

26 TUESDAY ☿ *Moon Age Day 17   Moon Sign Leo*

Start today as you mean to go on, even though you won't feel exactly on top form as the day gets going. Later on, though, the situation changes, with the Moon growing ever-closer to your own zodiac sign. By the evening you might be feeling ready to paint the town red, or at least a deep shade of pink.

27 WEDNESDAY *Moon Age Day 18   Moon Sign Virgo*

The Moon is back in your zodiac sign. This means a get-up-and-go sort of period and one that is typified by high levels of energy and an irrepressible desire to be out there in the mainstream of life. In terms of experiences, quality is as important as quantity, though you manage to get a little of both today.

28 THURSDAY *Moon Age Day 19   Moon Sign Virgo*

Future plans can give you a shot in the arm today. In fact, most Virgoans will be continuing the working week with a flourish and though not all news may be good, you can get the best from all of it. Rummage around to find clothes that you can put back into service because you are ingenious now.

29 FRIDAY *Moon Age Day 20   Moon Sign Libra*

The trouble with today is that there is a host of things to do and maybe not enough time to fit everything in. That's where planning is important. It is definitely better right now to do one task well than to botch half a dozen. If the weather is fair, a good walk would almost certainly do you good.

30 SATURDAY
Moon Age Day 21   Moon Sign Libra

This is a time of mental and physical efficiency, when it isn't difficult to say and do the right thing. Perhaps the only stumbling block comes in personal situations because romance isn't the best area of life for you today. Others can be grumpy and your partner may seem potentially difficult to deal with.

31 SUNDAY
Moon Age Day 22   Moon Sign Libra

There are some exciting and interesting possibilities in store for you at present. Look around you and see where life is taking you, because you can get much of what you want without having to try very hard. Convictions are important today, but don't take them to extremes.

February
2016

1 MONDAY
Moon Age Day 23   Moon Sign Scorpio

It's true that you have to work quite hard now to get the good things of life but being a Virgoan that doesn't worry you too much. Look out for the help and support of friends, some of whom have a good idea or two that, in the fullness of time, could make you significantly better off than you are now.

2 TUESDAY
Moon Age Day 24   Moon Sign Scorpio

Though you are more than ready to form new contacts of one sort or another today, you should avoid coming on too strong. Confidence is important, but you might give certain people the wrong impression. A healthy dose of your natural humility does more for you now than a brash approach.

3 WEDNESDAY
Moon Age Day 25   Moon Sign Sagittarius

Avoid spreading yourself too thinly across too many tasks today. It would be far better if you were to concentrate on one job at once and to do it properly. At home, you are especially creative right now and quite keen to build a more comfortable and pleasing environment, not just for yourself but for everyone.

4 THURSDAY
Moon Age Day 26   Moon Sign Sagittarius

Getting ahead today depends on a degree of specialised knowledge, which in one form or another we all have. Ask yourself what particular knowledge you have and concentrate on that. Your skills provide you with the ability to get on better and to make more money. Be supportive of friends who are in trouble.

5 FRIDAY   *Moon Age Day 27   Moon Sign Sagittarius*

The competitive side of your nature is stimulated by the presence of specific planetary trends. There's nothing especially wrong with this, just as long as you are thinking things through clearly and soundly. Don't give in to an impulse to overdo things, particularly when the jobs concerned are entirely voluntary.

6 SATURDAY   *Moon Age Day 28   Moon Sign Capricorn*

In a career sense, situations are beginning to improve, though it might be difficult to monitor this situation on a Saturday. This would be a good day for shopping or for spending some time in the company of lively and articulate friends. What you don't need at the moment is grumpy types.

7 SUNDAY   *Moon Age Day 29   Moon Sign Capricorn*

Although many of the opportunities that come your way today prove to be small in scope, the end result of them is likely to prove very positive. It is all a matter of looking carefully and then concentrating on one task at once. No matter how unlikely it looks, you can exert a greater influence over your own life now.

8 MONDAY   *Moon Age Day 0   Moon Sign Aquarius*

This is clearly a time of high spirits. Things that are going on in the outside world should lift your mood nicely. Freedom is the key to happiness and you will find yourself able to get through or over obstacles that have blocked your path for quite some time. What helps is that you are now being so realistic.

9 TUESDAY   *Moon Age Day 1   Moon Sign Aquarius*

Social matters ought to prove highly stimulating and you should be enjoying the company of a number of different sorts of people. You need to balance outside activities with pressing work obligations, in which you might be slipping behind a little. There should be plenty of time for enjoyment in the evening.

10 WEDNESDAY　　*Moon Age Day 2　Moon Sign Pisces*

You cannot get away entirely from the presence of the lunar low today. For a sign such as Virgo the position of the Moon in your opposite zodiac sign is not always particularly apparent. However, you may notice that life is not proceeding quite as smoothly as has recently been the case and extra effort is required.

11 THURSDAY　　*Moon Age Day 3　Moon Sign Pisces*

Once again, you will register the fact that things are not working out entirely as you might wish. An extra dose of self-created enthusiasm gets you through any minor difficulties now and there are new incentives coming your way before the day is out. The most promising aspects of your life are social in nature.

12 FRIDAY　　*Moon Age Day 4　Moon Sign Aries*

This is a very fruitful period for friendships and for finding people with whom you instinctively feel you have much in common. Some patience will be necessary regarding a specific enterprise but people probably won't keep you waiting too long. A degree of ingenuity is what is called for at this time.

13 SATURDAY　　*Moon Age Day 5　Moon Sign Aries*

Inside, you might be quaking at the thought of some contact or approach you now have to make, though this is absolutely necessary if you want to make more of yourself in the days and weeks ahead. Summon up all your courage and move forward. The people you fear are by no means ogres.

14 SUNDAY　　*Moon Age Day 6　Moon Sign Taurus*

Activities in the outer world should prove to be quite fulfilling. At the same time there is enjoyment to be found at home, so you could be quite torn as to what to do with your day. Decision making isn't difficult. Your nature at the moment is calm and steady, a fact not always typical of your zodiac sign.

15 MONDAY   *Moon Age Day 7   Moon Sign Taurus*

When it comes to professional matters, you can be quite successful this week. With tremendous perception and an instinct with regard to what is likely to work for you, it's time to put your best foot forward. On the romantic front you may find that new offers are on the way – that is if you are interested in them.

16 TUESDAY   *Moon Age Day 8   Moon Sign Gemini*

Your personality profile is running high and this is definitely the right time to go for what you want. Few people would refuse you at present, and where awkward people do crop up, your natural personality can bring them round in a flash. Conforming to expectations is boring to you now and you love to surprise people.

17 WEDNESDAY   *Moon Age Day 9   Moon Sign Gemini*

Someone is bugging you right now, and there appears to be very little you can do about the situation. It would be better by far to ignore what you cannot alter and to get on with something different instead. There are gains to be made financially, though certainly not through gambling or any form of speculation.

18 THURSDAY   *Moon Age Day 10   Moon Sign Cancer*

Financially speaking, there can be a few ups and downs at this time. All the more reason to spend wisely and after due consideration. This is a good time for romantic encounters, and especially so for Virgo people who are not already in a relationship. Others find you intriguing now.

19 FRIDAY   *Moon Age Day 11   Moon Sign Cancer*

Retrieving what you can from difficult situations, you make the best of everything today and won't be let down by the actions of your friends, one or two of whom prove to be extremely supportive. Create a friendly atmosphere whenever you can and be willing to put yourself out, even for a stranger.

20 SATURDAY
Moon Age Day 12   Moon Sign Cancer

Confidence remains intact for much of the weekend, though you might find one or two problems coming from the direction of family members. If this turns out to be the case, solve them as early in the day as you can. After that, you will feel the need for a change of scene and for social diversity.

21 SUNDAY
Moon Age Day 13   Moon Sign Leo

Rules and regulations are necessary, and you are not averse to inventing a few yourself on occasions. However, you don't always follow them and certainly not at the moment. There is an impish quality to your nature that allows you to wring humour out of any situations, professional, personal or social.

22 MONDAY
Moon Age Day 14   Moon Sign Leo

Confidence grows gradually, but certainly isn't at a height today. You may decide that the time is right to do some planning and to look ahead of yourself in practical issues. This is not really a day for taking risks, though this state of affairs is likely to change in only a short time. Make the most of the evening.

23 TUESDAY
Moon Age Day 15   Moon Sign Virgo

This can be a very good day for making progress. There are new inroads planned into special projects that are very close to your heart. Something you have been thinking about for a while can now become a reality and it clearly has financial implications. You don't really look for security today but will be in the market for excitement.

24 WEDNESDAY
Moon Age Day 16   Moon Sign Virgo

Although you are probably being very successful at present, this is no time for complacency. It is true that you have a superior sort of judgement but you need to use it in a very progressive manner. The outcome of recent efforts allows you to make more of yourself and to show an extremely positive face to the world.

25 THURSDAY
Moon Age Day 17   Moon Sign Libra

You still seem to be working well, but you need to be aware that not everyone around you is working to your advantage. Keep an open mind about friends who call on your support. Though you might think one or two of them have been foolish, you may still be prevailed upon to help them out.

26 FRIDAY
Moon Age Day 18   Moon Sign Libra

Almost from the start of the day it becomes obvious that some obstacles have been removed and that you are willing to pitch in and have a go at almost anything. Once again, you relish the change of pace, as well as new places and faces. A trip to the country or the coast might appeal.

27 SATURDAY
Moon Age Day 19   Moon Sign Libra

There are advantages about if you know where to look for them. Contrary to popular belief, things are turning your way financially, whilst the social scene should look extremely interesting at this time. When it comes to impressing those around you, actions speak louder than words.

28 SUNDAY
Moon Age Day 20   Moon Sign Scorpio

Sunday brings a change of pace. In areas of your life where things have been quiet, they now speed up, while in professional matters, there is a decline. Make the most of what life offers and be certain to show your partner how important they are to you. Changes to your home surroundings may be appealing now.

29 MONDAY
Moon Age Day 21   Moon Sign Scorpio

It's leap year day, and although not the most amazing time generally for Virgo, you can make much out of small opportunities you recognise. There is an ingenious quality about you right now, and it is something you should take notice of. Confidence hovers – sometimes very strong and on other occasions distinctly lacking.

March

2016

1 TUESDAY
Moon Age Day 22   Moon Sign Sagittarius

Give yourself a pat on the back for something you have recently achieved, but don't become complacent. In most situations, there is still a long way to go and you haven't wrung the best out of professional possibilities. Get a move on and avoid the slightly lethargic tendencies from which Virgo sometimes suffers.

2 WEDNESDAY
Moon Age Day 23   Moon Sign Sagittarius

This is potentially a time of small but regular increases where finances are concerned. Concentrate your effort in places and situations you know and understand. You show a strong willingness to help out others, especially friends you recognise to be going through a hard time at the moment.

3 THURSDAY
Moon Age Day 24   Moon Sign Sagittarius

Quick thinking and a general intellectual sharpness typifies your nature at present. Mercury is in a strong position, which inclines you to speak your mind in all situations. Some Virgo people began a health kick at the beginning of the year, the results of which are now definitely beginning to show.

4 FRIDAY
Moon Age Day 25   Moon Sign Capricorn

In a social sense, you should find plenty of light-hearted moments to pep up today. Work-wise, you are not in such a good position. It is possible that colleagues misunderstand your point of view and likewise teachers if you are in further education. Explaining yourself is vital at this time.

5 SATURDAY   *Moon Age Day 26   Moon Sign Capricorn*

It would be a good idea to vary your routines just as much as possible this weekend, without planning anything too much. If you remain flexible, all sorts of possibilities will find their way to you. People you haven't seen for some time could be turning up on your doorstep soon.

6 SUNDAY   *Moon Age Day 27   Moon Sign Aquarius*

Avoid getting carried away with issues that don't have anything directly to do with your life at present. Retain your energy for really important tasks because although you have plenty of get-up-and-go right now, it is easily dissipated. It's quality, rather than quantity that really pays out at this time.

7 MONDAY   *Moon Age Day 28   Moon Sign Aquarius*

The potential for attracting new people into your life now is very good. Although there is a definite shy side to your nature, it doesn't show very much at present. Most Virgo people will be young at heart, no matter what their age might be. Go for fun, because that's the most important factor now.

8 TUESDAY   *Moon Age Day 0   Moon Sign Pisces*

You won't be at your most energetic as today gets underway but you are in a good position to weigh up situations. Try not to have to make too many important decisions, leaving these until Thursday if you can. Relax and let others take some of the strain for the moment.

9 WEDNESDAY   *Moon Age Day 1   Moon Sign Pisces*

Enthusiasm is in short supply. You can do much better if you get some support and encouragement, particularly from your partner. Remember that anything you don't get done today will probably be achieved much more easily later in the week. It should be easy to find friends who are willing to spend time with you.

10 THURSDAY *Moon Age Day 2   Moon Sign Aries*

With your high spirits and energy soaring once again, right from the start of the day, it appears that you can achieve a great deal now. With any venture it would be sensible to strike whilst the iron is hot. It doesn't really matter in which direction you choose to turn your energies today because success is your second name.

11 FRIDAY *Moon Age Day 3   Moon Sign Aries*

You should be registering a genuinely light-hearted period, during which you find the answers you need almost without trying. If you do come up against the odd problem today, there is likely to be someone around who will solve it for you. The difference now is that you are not too shy or retiring to ask.

12 SATURDAY *Moon Age Day 4   Moon Sign Taurus*

Mundane and domestic matters can be trying, which is why you are looking for diversity in your weekend. Your confidence remains generally high, though there are people around who would change that situation if they could. Watch out for someone who wants to throw a spanner in the works.

13 SUNDAY *Moon Age Day 5   Moon Sign Taurus*

All areas of your life appear to be equally blessed at the moment, though the main accent has to be on practical and professional matters. If you have had some sort of idea in your head, possibly for earning more money, you really should take it out of the cupboard and look at it more closely now.

14 MONDAY *Moon Age Day 6   Moon Sign Gemini*

Certain people, most likely the ones with whom you work, can test your patience sorely today. For this reason alone, the focus of life needs to be pushed towards home, family and friendship. Assume for now that work is something you have to do, whereas your greatest pleasures lie temporarily elsewhere.

15 TUESDAY   *Moon Age Day 7   Moon Sign Gemini*

Both socially and romantically, there is much to captivate your interest now. It is possible that you are well ahead in your work, which ought to leave time for simply enjoying yourself. Consolidation is one of the most important tasks to Virgo people but is hardly of that much interest during such a spontaneous phase.

16 WEDNESDAY   *Moon Age Day 8   Moon Sign Gemini*

There are a few possible gains to be made today, some of which come as a surprise. This means you have to be ready for almost anything. Powers of communication are good at present and you can really make an impression when it counts the most. Don't be too quick to judge the wisdom of friends.

17 THURSDAY   *Moon Age Day 9   Moon Sign Cancer*

There are planetary aspects around now that favour a slightly rasher approach, particularly in terms of love and romance. You need to speak your mind, especially to your partner, particularly when you have something good to say. Nobody is going to be in the least embarrassed by your behaviour now, but nevertheless these actions are unusual for you.

18 FRIDAY   *Moon Age Day 10   Moon Sign Cancer*

As the working week draws to a close, there could well be a few tasks that have been left undone. You need to deal with these if you can and to clear the decks for further action on Monday. It is also important to make sure you won't have to worry about practical or professional issues during the weekend.

19 SATURDAY   *Moon Age Day 11   Moon Sign Leo*

Things might quieten down somewhat for today and tomorrow, but that doesn't mean you fail to take notice of what is going on around you. On the contrary, you really are keeping your eyes open and details that others don't see are immediately obvious to you. Don't be too rash with money right now.

20 SUNDAY
Moon Age Day 12   Moon Sign Leo

Some delays in favoured projects are inevitable now, which is why you have to exercise a little patience, particularly for today. Don't rush into anything, but use that capable Virgo brain and think things through carefully. A little preparation is worthwhile in any job you undertake today.

21 MONDAY
Moon Age Day 13   Moon Sign Virgo

The best of all planetary worlds is yours for the taking today and tomorrow. Not only do you have a really supportive Sun at the moment, the Moon is paying your zodiac sign its monthly visit. Go for gold this Monday, no matter what you decide to do. Very few people or situations will stand in your way.

22 TUESDAY
Moon Age Day 14   Moon Sign Virgo

If you don't get everything you want today, it certainly isn't through a lack of application. You can make most situations your own and influence greatly the way other people are thinking. Turn on the charm in the way you are doing at the moment and the world is your oyster.

23 WEDNESDAY
Moon Age Day 15   Moon Sign Virgo

Don't be too quick to jump to conclusions. There probably isn't too much time for thinking in any case. This is potentially a day of social events, and a period when you will not want to be tied down by too many routines. Your garden may be of special concern now, or open land, perhaps far from your abode.

24 THURSDAY
Moon Age Day 16   Moon Sign Libra

Give yourself a little time to become acclimatised to change, no matter how necessary it seems to be right now. The most difficult situation for Virgo people right at the moment would be to contemplate a house move. Even reorganising the furniture is something you will want to think long and hard about.

25 FRIDAY
Moon Age Day 17   Moon Sign Libra

The practical side of your nature is very much in evidence, but unless you are really sure about what you are doing, leave it until later. This Friday is best for planning, and for observing the way others do things. You need these periods of calm and quiet, in order to deal with the busier times that crop up regularly this year.

26 SATURDAY
Moon Age Day 18   Moon Sign Scorpio

If you find yourself facing some sort of social engagement, ensure you are fully prepared. Although you are a good public speaker, there is a slightly shy side to your nature and you have to overcome this now. Try not to fuss too much about details, as this is one of the less than perfect traits of your sign.

27 SUNDAY
Moon Age Day 19   Moon Sign Scorpio

Prepare yourself for a busy and fulfilling interlude. Some of your heart's desires are there to be fulfilled, just as long as you have good vision and show yourself willing to take the odd chance. Nothing was ever achieved in life without taking some sort of risk, and in your case they are always carefully calculated in any case.

28 MONDAY
Moon Age Day 20   Moon Sign Scorpio

Avoid getting involved in arguments today. Not only are most of them completely unnecessary, you don't stand much chance of winning out. Even if you feel you have scored a victory, it will be marginal to say the least. You don't actually have to agree with everyone, but neither do you have to deliberately disagree.

29 TUESDAY
Moon Age Day 21   Moon Sign Sagittarius

Don't put off until tomorrow something you can do perfectly well today. Time seems to stretch like elastic, allowing you to get masses done, and yet still leaving hours to spend in social pursuits or with your partner. Those Virgo subjects who are not romantically attached should keep their eyes open now.

30 WEDNESDAY *Moon Age Day 22   Moon Sign Sagittarius*

Although you are probably feeling generally good about life, it is unlikely that you can make the general headway you would wish at present. There are obstacles being placed in your path, though few of them are deliberate. The secret is to push on regardless and to remain optimistic.

31 THURSDAY   *Moon Age Day 23   Moon Sign Capricorn*

This is a day during which you want to concentrate on matters that are of interest specifically to you. If you can take others along with you, then so much the better, but your own sense of satisfaction is of utmost importance to you. Things that are old, curious or somehow mysterious could have special appeal.

2016

1 FRIDAY
Moon Age Day 24   Moon Sign Capricorn

A professional issue could cause a rather tense atmosphere today, unless you take it by the scruff of the neck and deal with it immediately. You need to be direct in all your dealings right now because hedging your bets won't work. Friends could display a disquieting lack of confidence in you, but try not to be disheartened.

2 SATURDAY
Moon Age Day 25   Moon Sign Capricorn

You will enjoy being the centre of attention wherever you go today. It would be a shame if the planetary aspects creating this tendency were wasted simply because this was nothing more than a routine day. Put yourself out to make sure there are social possibilities if you are working or tied up with domestic tasks.

3 SUNDAY
Moon Age Day 26   Moon Sign Aquarius

Practical issues and general run-of-the-mill situations are likely to take up much of your time today. Although you are likely to get plenty done, this probably could not be considered a particularly successful day. Creative potential is especially good now, however, so make sure that you utilise this in some way.

4 MONDAY
Moon Age Day 27   Moon Sign Aquarius

A financial issue is apt to prove somewhat complicated, leading you to seek the advice of someone who is more in the know than you are. Don't avoid discussions simply because you are not in a chatty frame of mind. Things need sorting out and you won't manage that without talking.

5 TUESDAY　　*Moon Age Day 28　Moon Sign Pisces*

The lunar low is almost certain to slow things down, though not disproportionately. All you really notice this month is the fact that things are not going exactly your way. If you stay away from material considerations and concentrate on having fun, the position of the Moon won't affect you at all.

6 WEDNESDAY　　*Moon Age Day 29　Moon Sign Pisces*

There are some tests of your patience to be dealt with today, but the same rules as yesterday still apply. Family matters are easy to deal with but you could find a certain restless streak beginning to develop within you. Go for anything that feels different but do stay away from taking undue risks for the moment.

7 THURSDAY　　*Moon Age Day 0　Moon Sign Aries*

Professional issues are now taken in your stride, proving once again how reliable you are, even when under some small stress. You can't expect everyone to agree with your point of view at the moment but in the end you will invariably turn out to be right. People should listen to Virgoans more than they do.

8 FRIDAY　　*Moon Age Day 1　Moon Sign Aries*

This is a really good day to be around the people you care for the most. Although you have been a distinctly social person on quite a few occasions this month, in the main you are happiest when you understand your surroundings and the people within it. Still, one or two friends prove to be positively inspirational.

9 SATURDAY　　*Moon Age Day 2　Moon Sign Taurus*

Having fun is likely to be your number one priority this Saturday. Although this is somewhat difficult in the midst of a busy life, you do presently have the ability to mix business with pleasure and to enjoy them both. Look for people who haven't been around recently and take the chance to have a chat.

10 SUNDAY
Moon Age Day 3   Moon Sign Taurus

There are some minor mishaps today, though most of them can presently be viewed in a humorous way. It is hard to take anything particularly seriously now and you really want to have fun. The practical joker within you raises its head and this facet of your nature continues for a few days at least.

11 MONDAY
Moon Age Day 4   Moon Sign Gemini

Coming to terms with a personal issue is part of what today is about. Be confident in your dealings with others and avoid giving anyone the impression that you are not certain regarding decisions you wish to take. Friends should prove to be especially helpful at the moment and genuinely do want to lend a hand.

12 TUESDAY
Moon Age Day 5   Moon Sign Gemini

It is towards the practical aspects of life that your mind now turns. You can discover a number of new ways to get ahead with your work and should also be enjoying the cut and thrust of an active life, particularly in areas that involve your colleagues. Family matters might have to be left on the backburner for a short while.

13 WEDNESDAY
Moon Age Day 6   Moon Sign Cancer

There is a chance today to broaden your personal horizons and to get on top of issues that might have puzzled you previously. Friendship is strong and people who have not played an important part in your life up to now start to become more significant. Look out for some unexpected financial gains.

14 THURSDAY
Moon Age Day 7   Moon Sign Cancer

Make this a good day for new input and ideas, some of which can really bring advantages into your life with the fullness of time. There are some fairly unusual circumstances about, leading to many coincidences and strange happenings. Most of these seem geared towards your greater success.

15 FRIDAY   *Moon Age Day 8   Moon Sign Leo*

You can't avoid the feeling that this is an 'off with the old and on with the new' time in your life. That's fine, but don't go too far just because you are on a roll. You would not want to accidentally abandon ways of thinking and acting that are not at all redundant in favour of ones that don't serve you as well.

16 SATURDAY   *Moon Age Day 9   Moon Sign Leo*

Get ready to take a starring role. Planetary trends are lining up once again to offer you a great deal of incentive. Although your practical progress could be marred because this is Saturday, you should have no difficulty whatsoever in making valuable allies. New friendships are likely to be formed at this time.

17 SUNDAY   *Moon Age Day 10   Moon Sign Virgo*

Almost anything you have planned for today will go well, and this is mainly because of the level of effort you are willing and able to put in. There is a strong element of luck running through most of what you do and this is definitely a time to back your hunches all the way.

18 MONDAY   *Moon Age Day 11   Moon Sign Virgo*

There are now great opportunities to make progress and ones that you will not want to pass by. Shopping today could lead to the discovery of genuine bargains, while social possibilities look particularly good. If there isn't much happening around you, the chances are you are not trying hard enough.

19 TUESDAY   *Moon Age Day 12   Moon Sign Virgo*

This could be another less than eventful day, but it is worth noting that this precedes a time that will be far more hectic. Now you need to clear the decks for action, making room for the active period that will come along during the later part of the week. Spend time with close, intimate contacts at the end of the day.

20 WEDNESDAY   *Moon Age Day 13   Moon Sign Libra*

Where decisions and methods are concerned you will show rather more circumspection today than you may have done yesterday. Now the innate caution of your zodiac sign shows, causing you to move forward very carefully. Any disputes still around in friendship circles can be quickly cleared up.

21 THURSDAY   *Moon Age Day 14   Moon Sign Libra*

Impressive socially, you find the world presenting you with enjoyable and stimulating company. Taking life in your stride, you should enjoy today and may find yourself making a great deal of personal offers and invitations. When it comes to romance, you are in a good position to show your lover exactly how you feel.

22 FRIDAY   *Moon Age Day 15   Moon Sign Libra*

You can make good progress at work today, but you could find your social possibilities rather limited. Little successes from the past begin to accumulate, and some ideas that have been at the back of your mind for a while can now be put to good use. Altogether an ingenious period, but also a slightly unsettled one.

23 SATURDAY   ☿   *Moon Age Day 16   Moon Sign Scorpio*

Where emotional ties are concerned, you need to be rather more careful than usual. It is easy for others to misunderstand what you are saying and to draw the wrong conclusions as a result. There are gains to be made through inventiveness and by being in the right place at the right time.

24 SUNDAY   ☿   *Moon Age Day 17   Moon Sign Scorpio*

There is now much to be gained by widening your personal horizons. Young Virgoans, or those looking for love, can expect opportunities to come along. Maybe you have an admirer you would never have guessed at – or perhaps you discover that a friend would wish to be very much more.

25 MONDAY ☿ *Moon Age Day 18   Moon Sign Sagittarius*

Today may find you streets ahead of others at work, or in any competitive endeavour. Don't fight shy of letting people know what you think. It is true that you are rather outspoken at the moment, but much of what you have to say makes a great deal of sense. Keep a sense of proportion regarding your spending.

26 TUESDAY ☿ *Moon Age Day 19   Moon Sign Sagittarius*

Now that the Sun is in your solar ninth house, you can expect a new phase to begin, during which the real you begins to show. The planets favour intellectual pursuits and your mind is working well. You may now address problems that might have taxed you in earlier weeks or months.

27 WEDNESDAY ☿ *Moon Age Day 20   Moon Sign Capricorn*

The potential for making steady progress is strong. At work, you should be able to address most matters well and would be unlikely to back down over issues you see as being important. Your personal life is likely to be settled, with romantic interludes permeating a generally sedate period.

28 THURSDAY ☿ *Moon Age Day 21   Moon Sign Capricorn*

A few emotional tensions could begin to surface now, leaving you feeling slightly wrung out. Although these have to be addressed, perhaps you don't have to take them quite as seriously as you do. Take heart from the fact that people are generally on your side, even if it doesn't always appear that this is so.

29 FRIDAY ☿ *Moon Age Day 22   Moon Sign Capricorn*

When it comes to general initiative, you won't be found in any way wanting on this Friday. At the same time, you need to take a close look around you. The summer is approaching fast, with the nights getting shorter and everything in the garden beginning to grow. Like the flowers, you need more space now.

30 SATURDAY   ☿ *Moon Age Day 23   Moon Sign Aquarius*

Don't allow the views of others to influence your own life to any great degree today. Of course, it is important to take on board alternative opinions, but that isn't the same as turning your world upside down to accommodate them. Remain interested and flexible, but only up to a point.

May

2016

1 SUNDAY
☿ *Moon Age Day 24   Moon Sign Aquarius*

Though you might be in the middle of a fairly busy schedule, there ought to be time to please loved ones and to make a fuss of friends. Co-operation at work can be worth a great deal and leads to better prospects for all in the end. You could be called on to supervise something, which brings kudos.

2 MONDAY
☿   *Moon Age Day 25   Moon Sign Pisces*

It would be best to keep your feelings out in the open today. Your zodiac sign has a tendency to bottle matters up on occasion, which is very rarely the right way to proceed. You could experience some small difficulty with mechanical gadgets of one sort or another and might have to enlist some help.

3 TUESDAY
☿   *Moon Age Day 26   Moon Sign Pisces*

The lunar low can cause you to falter regarding matters you were certain about just a short time ago. It would be sensible to remember that any negative feelings, today or tomorrow, are not necessarily representative of life as a whole. Take things steadily and don't try to move any mountains, not even small ones.

4 WEDNESDAY
☿   *Moon Age Day 27   Moon Sign Aries*

Today is definitely one of those times during which you get out of life almost exactly what you put into it. If you want to be lethargic, situations won't demand much of you but you won't make progress either. Better by far to go for gold and then to glory in the attention that comes your way.

5 THURSDAY ☿ *Moon Age Day 28   Moon Sign Aries*

In a general sense, you are likely to be very high-spirited at present. This attitude is infectious, as you are about to find out. Your popularity remains high and might actually increase. All the attention coming your way at the moment is great, but it isn't what Virgo usually looks for or expects.

6 FRIDAY ☿ *Moon Age Day 0   Moon Sign Taurus*

Better advancement is possible, probably because of all the effort you have put in recently. This doesn't necessarily refer to work. If you are a member of any particular organisation, perhaps you may be invited to take on a position of responsibility. In one way or another, the world seems to have confidence in you.

7 SATURDAY ☿ *Moon Age Day 1   Moon Sign Taurus*

Your ability to command attention and impress others could be put to the test today. With plenty going for you in a general sense and material situations still looking good, it's time to go for what you want. Although not everyone appears to have your best interests at heart, when it matters most friends come up trumps.

8 SUNDAY ☿ *Moon Age Day 2   Moon Sign Gemini*

Career issues should be quite fulfilling, even though so many Virgoans won't actually be working on a Sunday. What you can do is plan for later, though don't devote all of the day to this sphere of life. People around you clearly wish to have fun and the way you are feeling at present, you will want to join in.

9 MONDAY ☿ *Moon Age Day 3   Moon Sign Gemini*

Family matters should now be putting a smile on your face. Younger relatives especially have the ability to make you laugh, but so do many other situations and people because your sense of humour is so highly charged now. Plan for a different sort of week, with the possibility of movement and travel.

10 TUESDAY ☿ *Moon Age Day 4 Moon Sign Cancer*

The more widespread and different the company you find yourself in today, the better you are likely to feel. Abandoning for the moment thoughts of security and comfort, you may be seeking to put yourself to the test in a physical sense. Remember birthdays in the family and amongst your friends. This is a good emailing day.

11 WEDNESDAY ☿ *Moon Age Day 5 Moon Sign Cancer*

Your mind could turn towards creative pursuits of one sort or another. Yours is a very practical zodiac sign, so anything arty tends to have an everyday function for you too. Since you are an Earth sign, perhaps you might turn to something like pottery? There could also be some movement on the romantic front.

12 THURSDAY ☿ *Moon Age Day 6 Moon Sign Leo*

Travel and intellectual matters of all sorts are of specific interest to you at present, at a time when you won't take at all kindly to being tied down in the same place. If you can't get away right now, don't despair. Your mind is working overtime and you ought to be able to devise a strategy to get a break soon.

13 FRIDAY ☿ *Moon Age Day 7 Moon Sign Leo*

If it feels as though you are taking two steps forward and one back today, well at least you are making some sort of progress. You can't really expect to make too much of the running today and by Sunday you should understand why. A twelfth-house Moon always comes immediately ahead of the lunar high.

14 SATURDAY ☿ *Moon Age Day 8 Moon Sign Leo*

Address issues one at a time today and don't bite off more than you can chew. In the romantic department, it looks as though you are in for a very positive time. Those Virgo people who have been looking for love could enjoy a great deal more success now than has been the case for some days past.

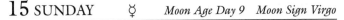

15 SUNDAY ☿ *Moon Age Day 9 Moon Sign Virgo*

Call in a few favours today because it is quite obvious that almost everyone is on your side. This is a Sunday to remember, or at least it will be if you only put in a modicum of effort. General good luck aids almost any enterprise you choose and relationships should be the cause of much happiness.

16 MONDAY ☿ *Moon Age Day 10 Moon Sign Virgo*

This is the time to put fresh ideas to the test. You won't want to feel in any way fettered and show a strong determination to do what pleases you. Since you are presently so charming, it is unlikely that anyone would deliberately stand in your way. Don't be afraid of some limited and carefully thought-out speculation.

17 TUESDAY ☿ *Moon Age Day 11 Moon Sign Libra*

You could find this to be a rather taxing time at work, leading you to be grateful once the responsibility is out of the way and you can finally please yourself. Socially speaking, you are on top form, which may be one of the reasons you are less professionally inclined just at the moment.

18 WEDNESDAY ☿ *Moon Age Day 12 Moon Sign Libra*

This is one of the best days of this month to enjoy what personal freedom surrounds you now. In some ways you could feel hemmed in by circumstances and will be keen to break down barriers as much as possible. Stay mobile and give your full attention to any situation that stimulates your mind.

19 THURSDAY ☿ *Moon Age Day 13 Moon Sign Libra*

In social matters especially, the impact of your personality is extremely strong at present. Do what you can to make a favourable impression, particularly amongst people who you know are on your side. There are some revolutionary ideas about at present and you are not shy about promoting them.

20 FRIDAY ☿ *Moon Age Day 14* *Moon Sign Scorpio*

Loved ones offer a definite dose of reassurance today, together with an ability to lift your spirits during the coming weekend. Friends too are important to have around and one or two of them have interesting things to tell you. Where money is concerned, suffice to say it is better to save than spend at the moment.

21 SATURDAY ☿ *Moon Age Day 15* *Moon Sign Scorpio*

Love-life and romantic matters show a definite improvement with the arrival of the weekend. This may be partly due to the fact that you have more time to concentrate on the needs of those around you, and particularly your partner. Don't be too quick to volunteer for too many jobs around the home though because these can mount up.

22 SUNDAY ☿ *Moon Age Day 16* *Moon Sign Sagittarius*

All sorts of outdoor pursuits would probably be right up your street now. The closer the real summer comes, the stronger is your urge to be out of doors and active. Follow your own ideas about how to have fun, but do it in the company of people you find amusing, educating and even charming.

23 MONDAY *Moon Age Day 17* *Moon Sign Sagittarius*

Communications generally are on the up and what sets the rest of this week apart is the very much better way you are able to get others to understand your point of view. Generally cheerful, you are good to have around and most of the people you know will be pleased to have you on board in any situation.

24 TUESDAY *Moon Age Day 18* *Moon Sign Sagittarius*

Whilst getting along with others in a career sense is a piece of cake today, things may not be quite so rosy in a personal or romantic sense. It appears that you are not able to tell people quite the way you feel, leading to misunderstandings and even disputes. Of course, it takes two to tango so remember that you don't have to argue at all.

25 WEDNESDAY   *Moon Age Day 19   Moon Sign Capricorn*

You think deeply and in a very capable manner today. This fact is not lost on others, who will be only too willing to seek your advice on a number of different topics. Try to stay active because long periods sitting and doing very little won't suit you, either in a mental or a physical way.

26 THURSDAY   *Moon Age Day 20   Moon Sign Capricorn*

It is your professional life that continues to be most rewarding at present. Good news is likely to be on the way that might also have a bearing on your romantic interests. Hold tight to money for the moment because the best bargains come along later this month. In the meantime, practice prudence over spending.

27 FRIDAY   *Moon Age Day 21   Moon Sign Aquarius*

A good time on the home front could help to alleviate slight problems now cropping up in other spheres of your life, particularly at work. Personal relationships ought to work rather well and offer you the chance to say things that might have been on your mind for quite some time.

28 SATURDAY   *Moon Age Day 22   Moon Sign Aquarius*

Social high spots are evident at the start of this weekend, with no desire on your part to stick around the house and vegetate. You would rather be climbing a high hill, or maybe looking out at a blue sea. All in all, this would not be at all a bad time to think about taking a holiday.

29 SUNDAY   *Moon Age Day 23   Moon Sign Pisces*

Although your mind is potentially geared towards your job today, many Virgo people will not even be at work. Instead, you need to think about movement of every conceivable kind. Sedentary pursuits won't appeal to you at all because you only want to be going wherever the mood takes you.

30 MONDAY *Moon Age Day 24   Moon Sign Pisces*

Your opinions are quite fired up at present, tending to make you rather emphatic in discussions. Be just a little careful because it is possible to cause offence without intending to do so. This is especially true if you are dealing with sensitive types, who don't quite know how to take your present attitude.

31 TUESDAY *Moon Age Day 25   Moon Sign Pisces*

The see-saw that is life is swinging again, bringing along a short period during which the charm you have been showing of late takes something of a holiday. You have to work hard today to accommodate those you really don't like, and to disguise the fact from both them and yourself.

2016

1 WEDNESDAY   *Moon Age Day 26   Moon Sign Aries*

Look out for a few ups and downs in your finances. You need to adapt more positively to outside circumstances and also possibly recognise a few limitations that are likely to be placed upon you now. In terms of personal relationships, this time should prove to be secure and can promote greater affection generally.

2 THURSDAY   *Moon Age Day 27   Moon Sign Aries*

This is a day for enjoying the social world and for communicating your ideas to others. You may need to concentrate because there is a danger that you are not seeing all situations the way they really are. Your confidence in your own abilities is on the increase and you might take chances today you wouldn't have considered yesterday.

3 FRIDAY   *Moon Age Day 28   Moon Sign Taurus*

You won't have to try very hard to impress anyone at the moment. However, compromise is a word you do need to keep in mind and there are no potential advantages to be had from refusing to adapt, even though your inner mind tells you this is the thing to do. All the same, impulsive actions may not bring rewards.

4 SATURDAY   *Moon Age Day 0   Moon Sign Taurus*

You can gain both emotionally, and perhaps financially, from the actions of loved ones. Your nature is warm and sensitive at present and you can be moved quite easily, perhaps by a memory, a piece of music or something that you have read. You may decide to look up people you haven't seen for a while.

5 SUNDAY
Moon Age Day 1   Moon Sign Gemini

Another boost comes along as far as your social life is concerned. If you get together with others, you can create an interesting time, once the concerns of the material world have been dealt with. You might also notice an upturn in your general fortune and financial strength, beginning at any time now.

6 MONDAY
Moon Age Day 2   Moon Sign Gemini

What you tend to deal with at the start of this working week is long-term plans and the strategies necessary to get what you want from your working life. Don't be too quick to jump to conclusions where the apparent actions of others are concerned. Give situations time to mature.

7 TUESDAY
Moon Age Day 3   Moon Sign Cancer

Your partner could now play a more dominant role in your life but only because that is the way you want the situation to be. In other spheres, you need to look very carefully at suggestions that are being made which somehow have a bearing on your working circumstances. Perhaps negotiation is necessary.

8 WEDNESDAY
Moon Age Day 4   Moon Sign Cancer

The current planetary trends may help you to latch on to any practical advantage that is around at the moment. Your confidence continues to grow, though the latter part of this week may see some small reversals. In a general sense, your life is moving forward, even though the progress is steady at present.

9 THURSDAY
Moon Age Day 5   Moon Sign Leo

A light and casual influence enters your life, thanks to the position of the little planet Mercury. You should find today to be uncomplicated and potentially enjoyable. Not everyone is going to be equally helpful, though you tend to stay away from the people who are not.

10 FRIDAY
Moon Age Day 6   Moon Sign Leo

You can't expect things to be exactly spectacular today. The Moon is in your solar twelfth house, making you more pensive and probably inclined to shy away from potential problems, if only for today. Routines might now seem comfortable and you are certainly in quite a thoughtful mood.

11 SATURDAY
Moon Age Day 7   Moon Sign Virgo

The lunar high this month has some very practical influences, which suits you down to the ground. You are strong and effective, both at work and at home. Changes you have been wanting to implement for some time now become entirely possible, and the more so if you show yourself to be dynamic.

12 SUNDAY
Moon Age Day 8   Moon Sign Virgo

This is a bonus period for personal relationships and for love especially. It won't be at all difficult to show your partner or sweetheart how you feel about them. Since the lunar high invariably brings better than average luck, it is also fair to suggest that you could afford to chance your arm in some small way today.

13 MONDAY
Moon Age Day 9   Moon Sign Virgo

The start of a new working week coincides with trends that particularly favour co-operative ventures of any sort. Be willing to put yourself out for the sake of the group as a whole, whilst continuing to plough your own furrow in other ways. Set out today to make sure that you don't find yourself completely out on a limb.

14 TUESDAY
Moon Age Day 10   Moon Sign Libra

You want to be in charge of financial matters now, even though others could disagree. What you must do is put forward a reasoned argument, explaining your point of view. If that doesn't work, leave things alone for a day or two. You need to leave time today to talk about less serious matters and to have fun.

15 WEDNESDAY *Moon Age Day 11   Moon Sign Libra*

Now you can make your move, both at work and in personal situations. To the outside world you appear successful and impressive, which means you are probably at the peak of your powers. Even if you don't feel entirely sure of yourself, it is the impression you give that means the most.

16 THURSDAY *Moon Age Day 12   Moon Sign Scorpio*

Good news could be coming in from a number of different directions, some of which prove to be quite unexpected. You should take these events in your stride and at the same time seek change and diversity in your life as a whole. Don't be too surprised if you are being singled out for special treatment.

17 FRIDAY *Moon Age Day 13   Moon Sign Scorpio*

Most matters can go your way today, with just a little effort on your part. If there are celebrations in the family, or within your friendship circle, there's a good chance you will want to join in. You have a fairly carefree attitude to life at present and can certainly enjoy all that romance offers.

18 SATURDAY *Moon Age Day 14   Moon Sign Scorpio*

Look out for a peak in terms of your professional life. If you are between jobs, or looking for something new, this would be a good time to keep your eyes open. Of course, this won't be as easy during the weekend, but timely chats with people who are in the know could still be useful.

19 SUNDAY *Moon Age Day 15   Moon Sign Sagittarius*

Don't believe everything you hear today because the chances are someone is deliberately trying to fool you in some way. Subject everything to your usual level of Virgoan scrutiny and give some thought to testing out one or two of your big ideas before you put them into practice.

20 MONDAY   *Moon Age Day 16   Moon Sign Sagittarius*

The things you learn today can be turned to your own advantage, so in addition to having plenty to say yourself, you are also keeping your ears open. Some Virgo people may learn things which bring them real power, mainly in a career sense. Do as much work as you can today because tomorrow needs to be more relaxed.

21 TUESDAY   *Moon Age Day 17   Moon Sign Capricorn*

Career developments can be aided by people who are in the know, though you also won't want to waste a second of what today offers romantically and socially. You are still riding high in the estimation of most people and are especially popular with those who see you as being a source of good advice.

22 WEDNESDAY   *Moon Age Day 18   Moon Sign Capricorn*

The greater number of people who make up your scene at present, the better you are going to feel. Don't be put off when you come up against a minor obstacle, but whatever you choose to do, keep moving towards your chosen goals. Speaking of goals, Virgo is generally very sporting at present.

23 THURSDAY   *Moon Age Day 19   Moon Sign Aquarius*

A new period of generally rewarding times is on the way, now that the Sun is in your solar eleventh house. You could be somewhat more contemplative, but that also means you are planning strategies more carefully. Avoid argumentative types, especially in personal and romantic attachments.

24 FRIDAY   *Moon Age Day 20   Moon Sign Aquarius*

Now you really are taking the starring role. Quieter times may be in store later but for the moment you simply love being in the limelight and won't be inclined to retreat into yourself at all. Still chatty, you could talk the hind leg off a donkey, and then start on the other legs too.

25 SATURDAY *Moon Age Day 21   Moon Sign Aquarius*

There are chores galore today, or at least that is the way it looks. Don't be too surprised if you are a little down in the dumps, though it is clear that matters lie predominantly in your own hands. Your creative potential is good but you could find obstacles being put in your path.

26 SUNDAY *Moon Age Day 22   Moon Sign Pisces*

Avoid taking risks with current developments. The lunar low could assist in removing some of the advantages you have built for yourself in the last week or two, so you need to exercise extra care today. Emotionally speaking, you are likely to feel stronger and generally more resilient.

27 MONDAY *Moon Age Day 23   Moon Sign Pisces*

The lunar low is still present but there are progressive trends in your chart, especially those dealing with social matters and ways of having fun. You might be slightly restricted in a material sense but that won't prevent you from finding enjoyment. However, you will probably feel more comfortable within your family.

28 TUESDAY *Moon Age Day 24   Moon Sign Aries*

It won't be too difficult to get your own way now, even with people who are tougher to crack than nuts. The fact is that you are seen as being very likeable and a good deal more flexible than is sometimes the case for Virgo. Acting on impulse is not really you but it does seem to work at present.

29 WEDNESDAY *Moon Age Day 25   Moon Sign Aries*

You appear to be in the middle of a generally beneficial period. What works best for you at the moment is talking. Virgo is strange, because it can be quite chatty or totally silent, it all depends on the day. For now, there is hardly a subject coming your way that you will fail to tell everyone all about.

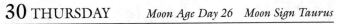

30 THURSDAY   *Moon Age Day 26   Moon Sign Taurus*

You have a far more determined approach to problem-solving now, and will actively be seeking out situations that you can turn to your own advantage. At the same time you naturally have a sensitive edge, which those you mix with the most could hardly fail to notice. You ought to be very popular around this time.

July

2016

1 FRIDAY
Moon Age Day 27   Moon Sign Taurus

If nothing else, the position of the Sun ensures a generally happy and carefree start to the new month. Group situations are well favoured at the moment, and you should not be at all surprised if you are pushed to the front. If you overcome your natural resistance to taking a position of authority, you can make a very good job of things.

2 SATURDAY
Moon Age Day 28   Moon Sign Gemini

You may be able to bend career situations your own way and stand a chance of making a good impression on others at the moment. You are certainly not lacking in confidence, though you could also discover that someone you counted as a friend is not doing you any favours. All the same, don't over-react.

3 SUNDAY
Moon Age Day 29   Moon Sign Gemini

You have a strong thirst for fresh experiences now. Seeking out change and variety in your life is likely to be extremely important and there are very few difficult trends to deal with today. Although you are still good at problem solving, you might have to seek out an expert during today or tomorrow.

4 MONDAY
Moon Age Day 0   Moon Sign Cancer

Career demands appear to be your main priority at the moment, though you should take time out to enjoy yourself too. Don't be too quick to jump to conclusions, particularly when dealing with people you don't know very well. You could be suffering from an over-suspicious nature today.

5 TUESDAY
Moon Age Day 1   Moon Sign Cancer

This could be a good day for family get-togethers or reunions of some sort. With a slightly nostalgic streak taking over, maybe you are looking on the internet to see if you can locate some of those buddies you haven't seen for years. If you find them, be prepared for one or two surprises.

6 WEDNESDAY
Moon Age Day 2   Moon Sign Leo

This is another of those periods during which you are happy to be in the social spotlight. Virgo is far more gregarious at the moment than would usually be the case. Don't panic because you still maintain that slight inner reserve that marks you out as being different from the showy zodiac signs.

7 THURSDAY
Moon Age Day 3   Moon Sign Leo

Today could be a day of emotional tensions, perhaps caused by the behaviour of colleagues. Although you demonstrate great loyalty this month, it won't always be coming back to you in the way you would wish or expect. Some situations may require a dose of intuition and common sense.

8 FRIDAY
Moon Age Day 4   Moon Sign Virgo

It's time to push ahead with your dreams and schemes because if you are going to make anything of them, this is the most likely period. Virgo may be feeling especially unsettled today, though not in a negative sense. Travel has been a distinct possibility over recent weeks, and is even more likely now.

9 SATURDAY
Moon Age Day 5   Moon Sign Virgo

Most everyday issues go according to plan and progress should be generally smooth. You can negotiate potential difficulties without really recognising they are present and should also enjoy a high degree of popularity in a general sense. Best of all, Lady Luck is likely to pay you a visit.

10 SUNDAY
Moon Age Day 6   Moon Sign Virgo

The more ambitious you are today, the better you are likely to be getting on. Keep your ears open because even the most casual of conversations could be carrying some surprising but useful news. In any situation, it can be quite crucial to strike while the iron is hot. At work, you are a force to be reckoned with.

11 MONDAY
Moon Age Day 7   Moon Sign Libra

A fairly cautious approach is necessary now where money is concerned, but the same cannot be said in the realm of romance. Here, Virgo is the king or queen. Without thinking, you heap so many compliments on the object of your desire that they will be putty in your hands.

12 TUESDAY
Moon Age Day 8   Moon Sign Libra

Your social life now seems to be the main focus of life. There are trends around at the moment that would make this period ideal for travel, so maybe a holiday is on the cards. Avoid allowing any of your plans to be altered by the attitude and opinions of people who are not really involved in them at all.

13 WEDNESDAY
Moon Age Day 9   Moon Sign Scorpio

Some of the problems you come across today simply cannot be overcome using pure logic. This is the usual first resort of Earthy Virgo, but you can be quite intuitive too, especially under current trends. Take a sideways look at situations and avoid taking the most obvious approach if it feels wrong.

14 THURSDAY
Moon Age Day 10   Moon Sign Scorpio

You are in a very good position to influence others. This applies particularly at work. Even if a degree of coercion is necessary, as long as you know the end genuinely does justify the means, you should go ahead. Once work is out of the way, you might be especially pleased to be out of doors.

15 FRIDAY   *Moon Age Day 11   Moon Sign Scorpio*

The most casual of meetings could turn into something much more interesting. Although there are one or two people around now who may not be trustworthy, it may not be at all difficult to see through these individuals. The most appealing thing about today is the sheer volume of work you can get through.

16 SATURDAY   *Moon Age Day 12   Moon Sign Sagittarius*

Although opportunities to get ahead are not plentiful, you recognise those that do appear and can squeeze through any crack to get what you want. Some people might accuse you of being sneaky and self-seeking, though the truth is that you have the interests of relatives, friends and colleagues at heart.

17 SUNDAY   *Moon Age Day 13   Moon Sign Sagittarius*

There are certain emotional pressures that you will have to work against today. Don't be too quick to push your point of view forward, particularly when you are talking to your partner or loved ones. Your confidence remains generally intact, but you can't be certain of bringing everyone on side now.

18 MONDAY   *Moon Age Day 14   Moon Sign Capricorn*

A much more progressive and positive phase is now at hand, with better potential advancements at work and a more determined attitude on your part. People you have not mixed with for a while might be making a return to your life soon, though some of these may be individuals with whom you have argued previously.

19 TUESDAY   *Moon Age Day 15   Moon Sign Capricorn*

Along comes a socially helpful period, during which those around you are more willing than ever to put themselves out on your behalf. Don't be too quick to judge the actions or opinions of a friend but stay flexible and even suggestible. Routines will bore you during this period, so avoid them.

♍

20 WEDNESDAY *Moon Age Day 16   Moon Sign Capricorn*

Teamwork and co-operative ventures probably have less to offer you at present than has been the case over the last couple of weeks. You are in a 'go it alone' frame of mind and that means having to rely more and more on yourself. The situation is rather different in terms of personal attachments however.

21 THURSDAY *Moon Age Day 17   Moon Sign Aquarius*

Avoid allowing yourself to be dominated by emotional impulses, particularly since many of them are not at all necessary. You need to free yourself from old habits and especially ones that you know are bad for you. With a forward-looking attitude later in the day, a greater contentment emerges.

22 FRIDAY *Moon Age Day 18   Moon Sign Aquarius*

You can't trust to luck today, but rather your own abilities. It might also be a mistake to automatically believe what others are saying. You wouldn't suggest, or even believe, that people are lying. On the contrary, they might be as much in the dark as you are and merely quoting possibilities.

23 SATURDAY *Moon Age Day 19   Moon Sign Pisces*

Whilst the lunar low is around it might be sensible to allow your partner or another family member to deal with some of the major issues on the home front. Although you can hold your own at work, you may not have quite the same feeling of progress that you have enjoyed over the last few days.

24 SUNDAY *Moon Age Day 20   Moon Sign Pisces*

Take things steadily today because there is a possibility that your life is beset with small pressures and issues that just won't work out the way you want. There is absolutely no point in becoming frustrated with the situation. In any case, by tomorrow everything should be on a more even keel.

25 MONDAY
Moon Age Day 21   Moon Sign Aries

You can't really expect to be number one today and if you take the time to consider why, then disappointments are less likely. This might be a good time for shopping, as long as you keep your spending moderate, and you may also be able to organise things very well, particularly in terms of working practices.

26 TUESDAY
Moon Age Day 22   Moon Sign Aries

The demands of your life make little indulgences less than likely at the moment. Circumstances force you into the limelight, a position you may not enjoy very much today. Don't be too quick to judge people or situations right now and listen very carefully to the thoughts of your partner.

27 WEDNESDAY
Moon Age Day 23   Moon Sign Taurus

Don't be afraid to consider specific changes to your life, if you know in your heart that they are going to benefit you later. Not everything goes your way today but you should be enjoying the summer and making the most of every opportunity to find fresh fields and pastures new.

28 THURSDAY
Moon Age Day 24   Moon Sign Taurus

This is a better time than most in which to keep your eyes and ears open for new chances of almost any sort. Creative potential is especially good and you instinctively know what looks and feels right. Moving outside your usual social mainstream, you probably feel more alive than has been the case for some days.

29 FRIDAY
Moon Age Day 25   Moon Sign Gemini

Getting away from any sort of rat race appeals to you at this stage of the week. If it's possible to take a long weekend, this would suit you best of all. However, the fact that you may be feeling somewhat withdrawn at the moment, doesn't preclude you from thinking up some startling ideas.

30 SATURDAY *Moon Age Day 26 Moon Sign Gemini*

Confused situations will follow if you put your faith in the wrong people today. It might be better to follow your own conscience in most matters and to stay away from deliberately provocative types. None of this prevents you from enjoying a generally happy and quite eventful Saturday.

31 SUNDAY *Moon Age Day 27 Moon Sign Cancer*

It would be best to opt for some light relief today and that is what you should be thinking about. There are substantial gains to be made where friendship is concerned and sociable associations with others could also lead to you discovering ways to get ahead in a financial as well as a personal way.

August 2016

1 MONDAY
Moon Age Day 28   Moon Sign Cancer

There is a strong emphasis now on broadening your horizons and on making sure you are in the right place at the right time to get ahead. Not everyone proves to be equally helpful today but if you turn in the right direction, you can be sure of the sort of support you are looking for.

2 TUESDAY
Moon Age Day 0   Moon Sign Cancer

Domestic responsibilities could so easily get in the way of things you would rather be doing. It pays dividends to think in advance and to make sure all those chores are out of the way so that you can concentrate on having fun. Compliments could be coming your way from unlikely directions.

3 WEDNESDAY
Moon Age Day 1   Moon Sign Leo

Conversations of all kinds should be appealing today. When they are combined with your present business acumen, you should be able to get ahead in a very positive manner. There is quite a restless streak about you and there is no doubt that there are times now when you would rather be travelling than staying around to attend to responsibilities.

4 THURSDAY
Moon Age Day 2   Moon Sign Leo

Your powers of attraction should be stronger than ever today. Compliments come your way from a host of different directions but nothing being said is likely to turn your steady Virgoan head. Intuition is strong, so you definitely know when someone is stringing you along, which could happen at this time.

5 FRIDAY
Moon Age Day 3   Moon Sign Virgo

The lunar high brings one of the high points of August. In today's bigger undertakings, you should discover that good luck is on your side and things just seem to fall into place. It should be especially easy to get your own way in group situations, and should remain so for a few days.

6 SATURDAY
Moon Age Day 4   Moon Sign Virgo

Press on with whatever activities you have planned and assume that things are going to work out the way you would wish. In the main, this is likely to be the case. This could be the best day of all for financial ventures and is also a notable period in terms of your overall popularity.

7 SUNDAY
Moon Age Day 5   Moon Sign Libra

There are many changes around just now and your greatest desire is to keep life on an even keel. Actually, it could be the case that you are trying too hard. Allow things to happen in their own good time. If you are constantly reacting, it is possible that you are not using enough intuition or your common sense.

8 MONDAY
Moon Age Day 6   Moon Sign Libra

Life has something of a mundane quality now. Nevertheless, your organisational skills are good and you can get ahead, sometimes against all the odds. In some jobs at least you could be far ahead of your intended position now, leaving you wondering just why you are working so hard.

9 TUESDAY
Moon Age Day 7   Moon Sign Libra

Keep on looking for those wide, open spaces. This is a holiday time generally but turns out to be an especially good time for you to take a break. If you cannot get away from the rat race, at least leave some time free at some stage during the day. Even a walk in the park would be better than nothing.

10 WEDNESDAY   *Moon Age Day 8   Moon Sign Scorpio*

Professional developments see moderate gains coming your way, though the real advances are being made before or after work. Socially speaking, you are on quite a high and enjoying all the attention that comes your way. Avoid any sort of petty jealousy, either inside or outside of work.

11 THURSDAY   *Moon Age Day 9   Moon Sign Scorpio*

Don't mishandle issues between yourself and someone who is important in your life. You need to be quite diplomatic today and to listen carefully to what is being said. On the financial front, it is possible that you are about to make an important decision but if you have already made up your mind, don't waver.

12 FRIDAY   *Moon Age Day 10   Moon Sign Sagittarius*

Life could take on a rather so-so quality today, unless you put in that extra bit of effort that can make all the difference. Don't be willing to accept second best, either from yourself or others. The urge to see new places is still around you and you might decide to make use of the coming weekend for travelling around.

13 SATURDAY   *Moon Age Day 11   Moon Sign Sagittarius*

Benefits come mainly from friends this weekend. You should find yourself well able to keep up with the few demands that are being made of you but there ought to enough time you can call your own. A mixture of activity and relaxation is what works best for you at the moment.

14 SUNDAY   *Moon Age Day 12   Moon Sign Sagittarius*

The escape you still want to make today could be either outwards or inwards. Some Virgo people show a definite introspective attitude towards the day and will be lost in their own dreams. The astrological circumstances today suggest you adopt whatever attitude suits you the best on a personal level.

15 MONDAY *Moon Age Day 13   Moon Sign Capricorn*

Socially speaking, you should be in for quite a happy day. Inwardly, you are less jittery and on edge than might have been the case during the last couple of days. Personal attachments flourish under the present planetary trends, bringing romance into the lives of young or young-at-heart Virgo subjects.

16 TUESDAY *Moon Age Day 14   Moon Sign Capricorn*

The charming side of your nature may come to the fore today, which is why you can be cheeky and get away with all sorts. Don't forget to keep in touch with family members who might be at a distance, and also with friends you haven't seen for quite some time.

17 WEDNESDAY *Moon Age Day 15   Moon Sign Aquarius*

Major decisions taken at work at present are best left to others for now. You are in a generally thoughtful frame of mind and might not be very keen to get involved in matters unless you are forced to. Dreamy Virgo tends to be a popular character, and you are far less fussy now than might sometimes be the case.

18 THURSDAY *Moon Age Day 16   Moon Sign Aquarius*

It appears that you are willing to stimulate the competitive instincts that are a part of your character. People can't get away with trying to fool you, and it is possible that you also take well to puzzles of almost any sort today. Once again, you feel the need to get out into the warm, summer air.

19 FRIDAY *Moon Age Day 17   Moon Sign Pisces*

Things are not moving quite a fast as you would wish, a fact that could lead to some small frustrations as the day wears on. Keep your eye on the ball, particularly when at work and don't allow others to steal a march on you. Your generally steady approach to life is an advantage.

20 SATURDAY
Moon Age Day 18   Moon Sign Pisces

Although the Moon is still in Pisces today, by the evening it moves on, leaving you feeling as if a great weight has been lifted from you. Almost immediately, you should be jumping about like a spring lamb. What matters most about today is the social possibilities that could occur by the evening.

21 SUNDAY
Moon Age Day 19   Moon Sign Aries

You now enjoy the company of a whole host of different sorts of people. Be willing to spend time with unusual types, who have a very different view of life from the one you generally hold. Don't get involved in family rows. You won't be starting them and haven't a great deal to contribute.

22 MONDAY
Moon Age Day 20   Moon Sign Aries

Look out for a slightly difficult day emotionally. You need to be absolutely sure that you understand what others are saying, and particularly your partner. As long as you are willing to talk things through steadily, then all should be well. What you shouldn't do is fly off the handle without being fully in possession of facts.

23 TUESDAY
Moon Age Day 21   Moon Sign Taurus

Strengths emerge, possibly with more force than has been the case at any time for weeks. You are a typical Virgo subject now, at least in a positive sense. This means you can write and speak well, and best of all, you have genuine 'command'. People won't argue with your decisions right now.

24 WEDNESDAY
Moon Age Day 22   Moon Sign Taurus

Put some ingenious ideas to the test and enlist the help of like-minded people whenever you can today. Don't be frightened to be out on a limb, or to make the most of situations that others think are past their sell-by date. You are a genuine original at present, and won't be afraid to show let people know it.

25 THURSDAY *Moon Age Day 23   Moon Sign Gemini*

Your ego is boosted tremendously, at what can turn out to be one of the most progressive phases during the whole of August. Be certain of what you want from life and then decide how to get it. Since there are so many people around who want to help you out, there is little chance of failure.

26 FRIDAY *Moon Age Day 24   Moon Sign Gemini*

You could be in the dark regarding information you have been waiting for. Take things steadily in a professional sense, but don't be afraid to paint the town red once work is out of the way. Any form of outdoor activity suits you down to the ground during this period.

27 SATURDAY *Moon Age Day 25   Moon Sign Gemini*

Friendly co-operation is what sets today apart. You can make gains through patience, perseverance and through being in the right place at the right time. Your intuition works strongly, and following it may lead you to all sorts of conclusions that might astound others. In a social sense, variety is now the spice of life.

28 SUNDAY *Moon Age Day 26   Moon Sign Cancer*

Sunday brings a slight slowing of the pace, though certainly not for long. In a social and personal sense you might not even notice this change in tempo. It is true, however, that you will be pleased to luxuriate somewhat, and you won't take kindly to being overwhelmed with work at the present time.

29 MONDAY *Moon Age Day 27   Moon Sign Cancer*

With regard to getting everyday matters sorted today, your attitude might be at fault. There are some tasks you simply don't want to undertake, it's as simple as that. Trying to get a Virgoan to do anything that goes against the grain is more or less impossible. Your stubborn streak is showing – but at least try to see the point of view of others.

30 TUESDAY   *Moon Age Day 28   Moon Sign Leo*

Close emotional attachments work better for you today than casual friendships or even associations at work. It might not be easy to see your way forward, particularly in a financial sense, but there are always people around who will offer sound advice and a helping hand.

31 WEDNESDAY ☿   *Moon Age Day 29   Moon Sign Leo*

Although your mind today might be almost anywhere except on the task at hand, there is a dreamy sort of quality to your thinking that feels very seductive. You can get things done, especially if you enrol the support of people within your family, or maybe friends. Subconsciously, you are on the verge of a breakthrough.

September
2016

1 THURSDAY ☿ *Moon Age Day 0   Moon Sign Virgo*

If you refuse to listen to others today, it's possible that you are doing both them and you a definite disfavour. Even people you haven't thought of as being the types to offer advice have some interesting things to say now. On a different note, you need to be sure that letters are posted and emails sent.

2 FRIDAY ☿ *Moon Age Day 1   Moon Sign Virgo*

Today the lunar high really comes into full force, supercharging your nature and making it easy for you to see the way ahead. If you are single and have been wishing to ask someone out, this is the time to do it. Those in longer-term relationships should be getting special support from their partners.

3 SATURDAY ☿ *Moon Age Day 2   Moon Sign Virgo*

You certainly intend to be heard today and you won't be backward when it comes to letting people know this. Do your best to make sure you don't cause any offence, even without intending to do so. The present position of Mars can take just a little of the charm out of your nature.

4 SUNDAY ☿ *Moon Age Day 3   Moon Sign Libra*

There are some potentially interesting encounters around during Sunday, though not of course if you insist on staying behind closed doors. Now you need to spread your wings and there are people around you who will be only too willing to take a trip somewhere special with you.

5 MONDAY ☿ *Moon Age Day 4 Moon Sign Libra*

The more variety you have in your life, the better you are likely to enjoy yourself today. The start of a new working week means scoring significantly more successes than was possible last week. Right from the start, enlist the support of people you know to have similar ideas to your own.

6 TUESDAY ☿ *Moon Age Day 5 Moon Sign Scorpio*

It is in your professional life that things really tend to go with a swing now, though you can't dismiss the possibilities that also exist socially, and in romantic attachments. Present trends make Virgo quite willing to learn at the moment so it may be that you are developing a new interest or skill.

7 WEDNESDAY ☿ *Moon Age Day 6 Moon Sign Scorpio*

You can't please all of the people all of the time, a saying that is likely to make real sense to you today. There are times when it is pointless trying and in the end all you can do is make certain you are doing your best. Even that might be disbelieved by some people but that's the way life is.

8 THURSDAY ☿ *Moon Age Day 7 Moon Sign Scorpio*

You are probably making a greater impression on some people than you think. This is especially likely to be the case with those who are your intended romantic targets. Virgo is not showy or particularly noisy but you can still let people know you are around. Your confidence is almost palpable today.

9 FRIDAY ☿ *Moon Age Day 8 Moon Sign Sagittarius*

Where communication is concerned, you have it within you to get the best from others today. You have a natural tendency at present to fight for the underdog but before you do make certain your support is justified in this case. There might also be slightly more money around than you expected.

10 SATURDAY ☿ *Moon Age Day 9   Moon Sign Sagittarius*

This is a time when you will be asserting your independence and making it plain to almost anyone that you want to plough your own furrow. Although there may be some slight opposition to your plans right now, in the main your obvious determination will resign others to your chosen course of action.

11 SUNDAY ☿ *Moon Age Day 10   Moon Sign Capricorn*

You have plenty of opportunity at the moment to simply be yourself. You might think that the real you is not all that interesting or inspirational but it's what others think that counts. Show some caution in business dealings and don't allow anyone to take you for a ride or you could lose money.

12 MONDAY ☿ *Moon Age Day 11   Moon Sign Capricorn*

You have certain duties to fulfil and not all of them are equally enjoyable. However, these should not take the edge off your ability to enjoy this Monday. Although the inclination to travel has been strong within you for some weeks now, today's tendency is more of a stay at home one.

13 TUESDAY ☿ *Moon Age Day 12   Moon Sign Aquarius*

Work and practical matters could provide a few frustrations today. The fact is that you can't make everything go the way you would wish and that won't please you at all. Your best area of focus today would be your social life, which offers far more in the way of enjoyment than employment presently can.

14 WEDNESDAY ☿ *Moon Age Day 13   Moon Sign Aquarius*

Things are looking up. Although there are still some problems around, you tend to deal with them quickly and efficiently. This will probably be the most successful day of the working week and offers you the chance to take on new responsibilities. Don't fight shy of showing what you can do.

15 THURSDAY ☿ *Moon Age Day 14   Moon Sign Aquarius*

Though you might feel slightly less in command today, the fact is that you can still turn situations around and won't have any trouble predicting the way others are likely to react. With plenty to play for in the financial stakes, you won't be taking undue risks but might be considering calculated ones.

16 FRIDAY ☿ *Moon Age Day 15   Moon Sign Pisces*

It might be best to suspend major activities wherever you can, at least until after the weekend. That means giving yourself more spare time, some of which you can spend building broken bridges, particularly in the family. The fact that not everyone is seeing eye to eye at present isn't your fault, but it might feel as if it is.

17 SATURDAY ☿ *Moon Age Day 16   Moon Sign Pisces*

Another slightly quieter day and definitely not one during which you should take any financial risks. Keep it light and steady, no matter what you decide to do. If there are parties going on somewhere in your vicinity, you will want to join in, despite the fact that your social skills seem somewhat diminished at present.

18 SUNDAY ☿ *Moon Age Day 17   Moon Sign Aries*

You could so easily find yourself in a prominent position today, so you will need to keep your wits about you. Being in the limelight is a double-edged sword for Virgo – you often like it but sometimes hate the situation. Fortunately, you are not feeling particularly shy at present.

19 MONDAY ☿ *Moon Age Day 18   Moon Sign Aries*

You should now be feeling buoyed up physically and ready to face whatever challenges come your way. Although you have perhaps been lacking in stamina in recent days, the situation is now reversed. Challenges are something you will relish and the busier you are, the better you are likely to feel.

20 TUESDAY ☿ *Moon Age Day 19   Moon Sign Taurus*

Your mind is sharp and your sense of humour definitely intact. This gives you the ability to get ahead of the game and to show the world at large what you are made of. Today is comprised, in part, of positive social encounters, most of which are geared towards improving your personal situation.

21 WEDNESDAY ☿ *Moon Age Day 20   Moon Sign Taurus*

A different approach to some very personal encounters is probably called for if you want to make the very best of them. Don't be too quick to judge the way others are behaving and stay away from contentious issues whenever possible. On a romantic level, you can overcome some obstacles.

22 THURSDAY *Moon Age Day 21   Moon Sign Gemini*

This is a good period for broadening your mind and for coming to new and quite revolutionary conclusions, sometimes about yourself. Keep an open mind with regard to the activities of certain friends, but don't be badgered into actions that genuinely go against the grain as far as you are concerned.

23 FRIDAY *Moon Age Day 22   Moon Sign Gemini*

Issues of personality do put you on the spot today, meaning that you cannot hide in the shadows regarding any matter you feel particularly strongly about. Don't be reluctant to speak your mind just because you know others won't agree with your point of view. If you explain yourself, you may be able to persuade others around to your way of thinking.

24 SATURDAY *Moon Age Day 23   Moon Sign Cancer*

You will probably have your work cut out today, trying to show people how much you care about them. In the end you might simply have to tell them one last time and leave it at that. Hopefully, anyone close to you will realise the truth in their own time. Life continues to be busy and financial prospects look especially good.

25 SUNDAY
Moon Age Day 24   Moon Sign Cancer

This looks like being a busy period in most senses, though you should remember that a little rest is important too. Be prepared to go that extra mile for the sake of friends, and also take any proffered opportunity to travel. Confrontation with colleagues is not to be recommended at present.

26 MONDAY
Moon Age Day 25   Moon Sign Leo

Some good fortune could potentially come your way now, and you should also be handling cash well. Looking ahead isn't difficult, leading to a shrewd but speculative frame of mind. You should also be on the receiving end of plenty of compliments, but don't allow this to cause confusion as to the way others think about you.

27 TUESDAY
Moon Age Day 26   Moon Sign Leo

Although you have plenty to do today, there are still potential gains to be made away from the mainstream of practical living. You should be quite satisfied with the state of play in personal attachments and also have the chance to make significant gains when it comes to acquiring both possessions and money.

28 WEDNESDAY
Moon Age Day 27   Moon Sign Virgo

Seek what you want from life and then go for it, even though you might be somewhat nervous about the potential consequences. At the same time, it would be good to pace yourself, because arriving at any winning post too far ahead of the competition gets you noticed in ways you may not have chosen.

29 THURSDAY
Moon Age Day 28   Moon Sign Virgo

The pace of everyday life is clearly quite rapid at present, so much so that you don't really have time to stop and take a breath. Be specific when conversation with others because if there is something you want, you need to ask for it plainly. Most people will respect your present honesty and integrity.

30 FRIDAY
Moon Age Day 0   Moon Sign Virgo

This is a time of steady but relentless building, both in a financial and a personal sense. As a result, you should be quite happy because the most positive associations of Virgo are given endless scope. Try not to be too fussy about details and stick to what you know when it comes to public discussions.

October

2016

1 SATURDAY
Moon Age Day 1   Moon Sign Libra

If you experience any personal restrictions today, you are likely to find these extremely annoying. The truth is that Virgo knows where it wants to go and won't take kindly to being prevented from doing so. All the same, you retain the essential popularity that is your usual lot.

2 SUNDAY
Moon Age Day 2   Moon Sign Libra

This is the time to ditch whatever has been holding you back. If this is going to prove awkward or embarrassing, you might have to think things through first. What you can't do is carry on down a road that definitely isn't the right one for you. Comfort and security mean a great deal by the evening.

3 MONDAY
Moon Age Day 3   Moon Sign Scorpio

It's time to get busy. With energy levels particularly high and a genuine desire to get things done, you can probably start very early in the day. Once the practical necessities of the day are sorted, it's time to go out and have fun. You probably won't stop moving from the time you wake up until the moment you go to bed again.

4 TUESDAY
Moon Age Day 4   Moon Sign Scorpio

Relationships of almost any sort can be emotionally uplifting but where love and romance are concerned, the world should be your oyster right now. Confidence is not lacking, though is represented better in personal rather than professional situations. You could be on the receiving end of a very special favour.

5 WEDNESDAY   *Moon Age Day 5   Moon Sign Scorpio*

You can't believe everything you hear today, even if in a few cases you wish you could. A good dose of scepticism proves to be necessary because there may be some tall tales around. Beware though, because just when you think everyone is talking nonsense, the silliest story of all might just turn out to be true.

6 THURSDAY   *Moon Age Day 6   Moon Sign Sagittarius*

Gaining more in the way of financial resources could be your main priority at present. Although it might seem at first that there is nowhere you can get more cash, a logical and methodical Virgoan approach should win out in the end. In social encounters, you tend to shine now.

7 FRIDAY   *Moon Age Day 7   Moon Sign Sagittarius*

Important discussions or negotiations can turn up trumps for you today and could lead you to finding a way forward professionally that hasn't been an option before. Talk, talk and more talk is what matters for Virgo today because that's the only way you are going to alter anything.

8 SATURDAY   *Moon Age Day 8   Moon Sign Capricorn*

Because there is much to get done today, specific issues may have to be re-routed or even changed altogether. There could be a feeling of dislocation and a tendency to fight shy of things you don't want to face. It would be sensible to talk to someone who is in the know, especially if their advice is usually sound.

9 SUNDAY   *Moon Age Day 9   Moon Sign Capricorn*

Your sense of adventure is strong this Sunday. You almost certainly will not want to stay at home and put your feet up. This is the sort of period during which you set yourself a challenge and then go out and achieve it. Advice from others may be well intentioned but you probably don't want it at all.

10 MONDAY   *Moon Age Day 10   Moon Sign Capricorn*

Happy encounters with people from the past are quite likely to take place at any time now. There is a sense of nostalgia about that is difficult to define, yet which could certainly be of use if you view it positively. One thing is for sure, you should not dwell on the past because that could lead to unfair comparisons in your mind.

11 TUESDAY   *Moon Age Day 11   Moon Sign Aquarius*

Getting what you want, either in a professional or a personal sense should not prove to be at all difficult now. You have strong willpower and a determination that presently cannot be bettered by any other zodiac sign. Decide what you want from life and find ways to gain your objectives that are unique.

12 WEDNESDAY   *Moon Age Day 12   Moon Sign Aquarius*

You show great efficiency today and can be sure that whatever you tackle gets done well and quickly. Don't be at all surprised if your popularity is going off the scale and make the most of the improving social trends. There are some very talkative people around at the moment and you are not the least of them.

13 THURSDAY   *Moon Age Day 13   Moon Sign Pisces*

It might be best to allow others to take some of the decisions, at least during the current lunar low. It won't be easy to make any real progress and you need the advice and support that others can offer in order to make the very best of the day. The main problem is that everything seems to take so long.

14 FRIDAY   *Moon Age Day 14   Moon Sign Pisces*

Your general capabilities are not up to scratch, or at least that's the way it seems from your perspective. Actually, you are probably doing a great deal better than you realise. Towards the end of the day you should discover that things are brightening up generally but don't take any undue risks all the same.

15 SATURDAY   *Moon Age Day 15   Moon Sign Aries*

The desire you are presently feeling to broaden your horizons could prove to be a very good incentive at this time. Few situations should be holding you back from this morning on, though you are likely to encounter some difficulty with younger family members, wayward friends and possibly a person who often embarrasses you.

16 SUNDAY   *Moon Age Day 16   Moon Sign Aries*

This is a time during which love life and relationships should be putting a very definite smile on your face. If you don't have the time to do everything you wish in a practical sense, be willing to leave some of it for another day. Most of the people you meet today prove to be very reasonable.

17 MONDAY   *Moon Age Day 17   Moon Sign Taurus*

You are at your very best now in small gatherings, and especially so when mixing with people you already know. The slightly shyer side of Virgo is showing and you also demonstrate a reserve that casual acquaintances might not understand. Nevertheless, in a professional sense you still display confidence.

18 TUESDAY   *Moon Age Day 18   Moon Sign Taurus*

Don't believe everything you hear today because there are some fibbers around. Mostly these will represent people who are charming and quite incapable of doing you any harm, but you need to be on your guard all the same. The planets suggest that you could also be temporarily affected by some mysterious little illnesses or setbacks.

19 WEDNESDAY   *Moon Age Day 19   Moon Sign Gemini*

Today could be a mixed bag, but is still likely to favour you in a general sense. If there are any frustrations, these are likely to come about as a result of the attitude of colleagues, some of whom are ploughing a very different furrow from your own. Keep abreast of things that are happening in your immediate locality.

20 THURSDAY   *Moon Age Day 20   Moon Sign Gemini*

Work and practical affairs keep you generally busy today and offer you the comfort of knowing that life is running in a smooth and steady way. There probably won't be too much in the way of excitement, though you are hardly likely to be fazed by that fact at the moment.

21 FRIDAY   *Moon Age Day 21   Moon Sign Cancer*

You could discover that in financial matters you have to take a very patient point of view, which could make it difficult to act with immediacy. This can lead to some inner conflict because you really do want to get ahead today. Your creative potential remains essentially high, with some wonderful ideas coming along.

22 SATURDAY   *Moon Age Day 22   Moon Sign Cancer*

Everyday life is apt to be pleasant and rewarding, with personal relationships offering the best possibilities of all this Saturday. You can make life go with a swing for family members, and most of all for your partner. It should also be possible to speculate rather more than you have been doing earlier in the week.

23 SUNDAY   *Moon Age Day 23   Moon Sign Leo*

The lunar high for October carries a promise of better luck and an ability to see through what might look like the 'fog' of life, clear to the heart of situations. You know what you want from life at the moment and what's even better is that you have a fairly good idea how you are going to get it.

24 MONDAY   *Moon Age Day 24   Moon Sign Leo*

You are presently enjoying a high profile at present, leading you to take a few chances that you would shy away from under normal circumstances. Where there have been problems in your life, you tend to address them methodically but consistently, which could mean that you soon demolish a whole pile of minor concerns.

25 TUESDAY
Moon Age Day 25   Moon Sign Leo

A number of different necessities keep you busy and on the move. Significant progress should be the result, which itself leads to feelings of great satisfaction later in the day. At least a few hours today should be spent relaxing, probably in the company of people you haven't seen as much of as you would wish.

26 WEDNESDAY
Moon Age Day 26   Moon Sign Virgo

Much in life should be going your way today and the lunar high helps you to get ahead in a profitable way. Whether or not this profit is financial in nature remains to be seen. Bearing in mind other trends it is far more likely that you are gaining credibility and popularity in the eyes of others.

27 THURSDAY
Moon Age Day 27   Moon Sign Virgo

Although you are feeling quite assertive today, you do need to watch your step in some ways. Not everyone is working towards your ultimate good, no matter what they say to the contrary. Problems are not likely to arise with relatives or friends, though colleagues could be more of a problem.

28 FRIDAY
Moon Age Day 28   Moon Sign Libra

Trends today suggest that you should find work reasonably fulfilling, but that your social and personal life should be better still. Romance seems to raise its head on a number of occasions, especially if you put yourself out. This might be a good time to buy someone a bunch of flowers or some other small gift.

29 SATURDAY
Moon Age Day 29   Moon Sign Libra

Good times in relationships mark the weekend out as feeling safe, warm and generally comfortable. Although you can't count on the support of everyone you know, in the main the people you rely on the most come up trumps on your behalf. Concentrate on issues that can make you better off financially.

30 SUNDAY
Moon Age Day 0   Moon Sign Libra

Beware of problems regarding money. You should be very careful what you spend today, and the things you spend it on. All in all, it might be best not to over-extend yourself financially at this point in time, but instead save and look ahead. You won't be too conservative in other ways, however.

31 MONDAY
Moon Age Day 1   Moon Sign Scorpio

Getting out and about, away from routines, does wonders for your attitude at present. Outdoor pursuits would suit you fine, and you won't worry too much about what the weather decides to do. If circumstances keep you rooted to the spot, you will need to turn up the level of your imagination instead.

November 2016

1 TUESDAY
Moon Age Day 2   Moon Sign Scorpio

Today should be very enjoyable from a social point of view, even if you can't get everything you want in a material sense. In a way, that won't matter because the most important gifts that come to you now cost nothing in monetary terms. It is impossible to put a price on love, respect and genuine affection.

2 WEDNESDAY
Moon Age Day 3   Moon Sign Sagittarius

When it comes to making decisions at the moment you can't take anything for granted. Look at situations carefully and take some advice from people in the know if it is offered. Generally speaking, you want to enjoy what the middle of the week has to offer, most likely in the company of your partner or a good friend.

3 THURSDAY
Moon Age Day 4   Moon Sign Sagittarius

Opt for some light relief if possible. You are in a state of mind that makes it impossible for you to take yourself or anyone else very seriously. There are gains coming as a result of things you did in the past. This might cause you to look back and adopt a previous strategy again.

4 FRIDAY
Moon Age Day 5   Moon Sign Sagittarius

All of a sudden Virgo becomes very competitive. This is thanks to the present position of the planet Mars and it does mean that you want to reach the winning post first in almost any situation. You remain essentially co-operative and believe in teamwork, just as long as you are in charge of the team!

5 SATURDAY　　　*Moon Age Day 6　Moon Sign Capricorn*

You may find it hard to communicate matters to others at the moment. People can so often get the wrong end of the stick and this is partly because you do not explain yourself well enough. Review past events if you must, but don't allow yourself to dwell on them so much that they get in the way of present decisions.

6 SUNDAY　　　*Moon Age Day 7　Moon Sign Capricorn*

Getting to grips with facts and figures might not be very inviting today but it could be necessary all the same. There are jobs to do that you really don't want to tackle but in the end you do them with good grace early in the day, if only to get them out of the way so that you can have fun.

7 MONDAY　　　*Moon Age Day 8　Moon Sign Aquarius*

There are many good things likely to happen around you today, not least in professional matters. Although this is an area of life that can take up a good deal of time it probably isn't the most important area to you. In the end it is relationships that capture your imagination the most.

8 TUESDAY　　　*Moon Age Day 9　Moon Sign Aquarius*

Clear communication is necessary if you want to enjoy a successful life early this week. Make sure others know perfectly well what you are saying, and why. On another front, you might notice that there are many personal compliments coming your way, perhaps from interesting directions.

9 WEDNESDAY　　　*Moon Age Day 10　Moon Sign Pisces*

A fairly sluggish day is on the cards and a time when it might be difficult to get what you want from situations. To a great extent, you can blame the arrival of the lunar low. What won't help is to push on against all the odds. It would be far better to take a rest and come out fighting in a couple of days.

10 THURSDAY *Moon Age Day 11 Moon Sign Pisces*

This is likely to be another day on which it will be impossible to get your own way in everything. Simply watch and wait, biding your time and laying down plans that you can action as soon as tomorrow. Confidence might seem to be lacking at present but this is only a very temporary glitch.

11 FRIDAY *Moon Age Day 12 Moon Sign Pisces*

You can probably look forward to a little ego boost in social encounters because some compliments are likely to be coming your way. Under present circumstances this situation is hardly likely to turn your head but it is good to know that people notice you and want to be pleasant.

12 SATURDAY *Moon Age Day 13 Moon Sign Aries*

There is little real scope for your ego to show itself very much at this stage of the week. It isn't out of the question that you will feel slightly dispirited and inclined to retreat into your shell somewhat. The planetary trends creating this interlude are very short-lived and so slight you may not notice them at all.

13 SUNDAY *Moon Age Day 14 Moon Sign Aries*

Compromises don't come easy to you now and you will have to try that little bit harder to deal with behaviour and attitudes you don't entirely understand. What you can be sure of today is that the future looks generally brighter and that you are now socialising more than of late.

14 MONDAY *Moon Age Day 15 Moon Sign Taurus*

This should be a socially favourable day and one during which you can enhance your financial wherewithal, simply by saying and doing the right things. Don't get hung-up on specifics because it is the broad cross-section of life that matters at the moment. It might have occurred to you for the first time today that Christmas is not far away.

15 TUESDAY
Moon Age Day 16   Moon Sign Taurus

Though certain invitations come your way this Tuesday, there is something in your mood that makes you a less socially-inclined animal for the moment. This doesn't mean you are avoiding other people but merely that part of your time is spent alone. Keep an open mind about some of your recently-hatched schemes and ideas.

16 WEDNESDAY
Moon Age Day 17   Moon Sign Gemini

You are in the mood for luxury, and when such feelings come upon Earthy Virgo, there is nothing for it but to treat yourself somehow. See if you can get someone else to do the housework today, whilst you pamper yourself with a massage or a session at the health centre.

17 THURSDAY
Moon Age Day 18   Moon Sign Gemini

You will have to fall back on your own wits today because the people around you may not be reliable. The problem is that you have very exacting standards at present and won't be too keen to relinquish control in any case. Be prepared to alter your ideas when circumstances don't turn out as you may have expected.

18 FRIDAY
Moon Age Day 19   Moon Sign Cancer

The generally lucrative period continues, though you won't have everything you would wish today. Part of the reason for this is that some of your expectations are not entirely realistic. This only leads to disappointments if you fail to realise how life really is. A more contemplative phase is needed.

19 SATURDAY
Moon Age Day 20   Moon Sign Cancer

Your mind works swiftly, leading you to arrive at some quite staggering conclusions, often on the spur of the moment. The start of the weekend makes specific demands of you, and especially so in a practical sense. You may be quite pleased to lay down some responsibilities by the evening.

20 SUNDAY   *Moon Age Day 21   Moon Sign Leo*

Getting your own way in financial matters could be surprisingly easy, probably leading you to be rather suspicious about others. A little mild paranoia on occasions is part of the Virgo nature, though it probably isn't at all warranted right now. Create some space to spend a few hours on your own.

21 MONDAY   *Moon Age Day 22   Moon Sign Leo*

You feel good about yourself and life in general as the week gets started. There is tremendous scope for advancement at work, plus extra incentive to go out and get what you want. Although you will come across obstacles at some stage during the day, these are unlikely to hold you back.

22 TUESDAY   *Moon Age Day 23   Moon Sign Virgo*

The green light is on and you are feeling positive and dynamic. Not everyone is in the same state of mind that you are, a fact that means maybe leaving others to catch up later. Quick on the uptake and certainly anxious to make the most of romantic possibilities, the world is your oyster right now.

23 WEDNESDAY   *Moon Age Day 24   Moon Sign Virgo*

There are few – if any – obstacles to your progress in life at the moment. Enjoying the best of all worlds, you should be responsive to change and anxious to follow situations through to their logical conclusions. If there are tensions to deal with, now is the right time to address them.

24 THURSDAY   *Moon Age Day 25   Moon Sign Libra*

Once again, you are struck by a burning need for luxuries of one sort or another. Virgo is quite insecure and owning new things feeds your self-esteem. Of course, they aren't really necessary but as long as you don't break the family bank you can probably afford to indulge yourself a little.

25 FRIDAY
Moon Age Day 26   Moon Sign Libra

It is easier to get what you want from life now but, as is typical of your nature, you probably won't want it any more. It's the simpler things in life that appeal most at present, for example the company of good friends and being able to enjoy a well-cooked meal. Your social trends are looking good.

26 SATURDAY
Moon Age Day 27   Moon Sign Libra

A few obstacles could prevent you from making quite as much of this Saturday as you would wish. However, if you set your stall out carefully, you should be able to get away with barely noticing any slight problems. This would not be a good day to climb a mountain or to take part in other vigorous exercise.

27 SUNDAY
Moon Age Day 28   Moon Sign Scorpio

You have little real patience with particular emotional problems today and you may consider that someone you know well is acting in a fairly irrational manner. There are some unusual people about, whose ideas and actions could fascinate you somewhat – but don't be drawn into anything weird.

28 MONDAY
Moon Age Day 29   Moon Sign Scorpio

Personal concerns or wishes can be successfully addressed today, possibly partly as a result of information that comes through the post or over the internet. Concern for your friends is also apparent, as you try to help someone sort out a thorny problem associated with relationships.

29 TUESDAY
Moon Age Day 0   Moon Sign Sagittarius

The everyday routines of life should become more interesting now and it is clear you are taking notice of situations that have previously passed you by for one reason or another. New interests could follow and you show a greater than usual concern for practical matters, especially in the way they have a bearing on your own circumstances.

30 WEDNESDAY *Moon Age Day 1* *Moon Sign Sagittarius*

You will want to maintain a fast pace of life and won't easily be put off by people who you see as a wet blanket. Concern for relatives is evident, maybe as a result of actions they are taking with which you cannot agree. Conforming to expectations yourself may also not be easy at present.

December

2016

1 THURSDAY
Moon Age Day 2   Moon Sign Sagittarius

The main thing today is to keep on top of organisational issues. You won't be very pleased with yourself if situations become confused or if you are not keeping up with the expectations others have of you. In a more general sense, you ought to be feeling quite positive about life.

2 FRIDAY
Moon Age Day 3   Moon Sign Capricorn

Career developments should now be going your way, though on a day that has much to recommend it in terms of sociability and general events, work could be the last thing on your mind. Even casual conversations with others can lead you to far-reaching conclusions.

3 SATURDAY
Moon Age Day 4   Moon Sign Capricorn

The spirit of teamwork is strong in you today and your ability to get on well with the world at large is particularly noticeable. Specific planetary trends show this to be a time during which Virgo becomes fascinated by the way things work. Some experimentation is called for, if only to satisfy your curiosity.

4 SUNDAY
Moon Age Day 5   Moon Sign Aquarius

Teamwork issues remain rewarding today and it looks as though you are becoming the life and soul of the party. Active and inspirational, you respond very well to changing circumstances and will now be more willing to actually inject a degree of uncertainty and even risk into your life.

5 MONDAY
Moon Age Day 6   Moon Sign Aquarius

Although friends could have a confused attitude towards specific situations, your own mind is crystal clear and you have little or no difficulty in organising yourself and others. The social aspects of Christmas might have started for you already, which is no bad thing when you are feeling so positive.

6 TUESDAY
Moon Age Day 7   Moon Sign Aquarius

Gathering together all the relevant information you need should be child's play now. You are particularly well organised at the moment, which is probably why others turn to you when they need sorting out. It might be necessary to fend off one or two social invitations, if only because you can't do everything.

7 WEDNESDAY
Moon Age Day 8   Moon Sign Pisces

You may feel slightly unlucky today, in which case it would be best not to chance your arm. Take any opportunity to relax a little. If you are able to find ways to cosset yourself, or perhaps are lucky enough to be able to sink into the lap of luxury, you will hardly notice the lunar low at all!

8 THURSDAY
Moon Age Day 9   Moon Sign Pisces

There are great rewards to be had from even the most mundane situations, though you will have to look at matters carefully and use a good deal of intuition to get the best from any situation. It might just be that you feel you cannot break through the carefully crafted shell of a colleague or friend.

9 FRIDAY
Moon Age Day 10   Moon Sign Aries

Though your career ambitions might have rather less going for them than has been the case lately, you should certainly be enjoying yourself in terms of your personal life. Compliments are easy to come by and you are likely to turn heads wherever you go, especially by the evening.

10 SATURDAY
Moon Age Day 11   Moon Sign Aries

The circumstances surrounding your home life and domestic issues generally seem to be going your way. There is a great sense of comfort and security about now, mixed with a tinge of nostalgia, probably on account of the time of year. Despite this, you must be realistic.

11 SUNDAY
Moon Age Day 12   Moon Sign Taurus

If at all possible, avoid potentially deceptive situations this Sunday. If you are about to sign a document, read the small print very carefully. It isn't often that Virgo is duped or fooled and once you realise that this is a possibility today, you will be on your guard. Family relationships and interaction might make you laugh.

12 MONDAY
Moon Age Day 13   Moon Sign Taurus

Personal and intimate matters are the most rewarding of all this Monday. You will be quite busy in a moment-by-moment sense, but you need to spare some time to show your lover how much you care. The response you get is very positive and should see you finishing the day on a high note.

13 TUESDAY
Moon Age Day 14   Moon Sign Gemini

It isn't difficult for you to maintain a high profile in most situations at this stage of the working week. Many Virgo people will be putting thoughts of Christmas on hold, opting instead for the chance to get ahead in a professional sense. People really do want to hear what you are saying at present.

14 WEDNESDAY
Moon Age Day 15   Moon Sign Gemini

Although today could begin fairly steadily, things should soon heat up. Progress is hard to see at first, which is why, by lunchtime, you have to put in that extra bit of effort that can make all the difference. By the evening you can be the life and soul of any party. If there isn't one on offer you might create a shindig yourself.

15 THURSDAY *Moon Age Day 16   Moon Sign Cancer*

Things change yet again, and you may be in such a hurry to get things done, you are in danger of forgetting some of the most important details. If you want to avoid having to stop, and then begin all over again, you need to concentrate. Friends can lend a helping hand if you offer them the chance to do so.

16 FRIDAY *Moon Age Day 17   Moon Sign Cancer*

A sense that you can rely only on yourself might prevail today. Up to a point that might be the case, but you ought to give friends the benefit of the doubt all the same. Offer others a helping hand in specific tasks that are familiar to you, but don't get in the way if younger people are seeking independence.

17 SATURDAY *Moon Age Day 18   Moon Sign Leo*

Beware a heavy-handed approach at home, particularly with younger people, who are only seeking to spread their wings. You should learn to trust, as others are willing to trust you. Only in the rarest of circumstances are you likely to be let down. The confidence to do the right thing is there, but you need to look for it.

18 SUNDAY *Moon Age Day 19   Moon Sign Leo*

Financially speaking, there could be some minor improvements now, and not a moment too soon with Christmas so close. Nevertheless, you need to spend wisely and to look out for those bargains that lie around every corner. All in all, this could be one of the best days of December for shopping.

19 MONDAY *Moon Age Day 20   Moon Sign Virgo*

As the month advances, so you begin to realise with startling clarity that Christmas is just around the corner. That won't be any problem today or tomorrow because you have more than enough energy to organise things. The lunar high makes you feel very positive about most situations now.

20 TUESDAY ☿ *Moon Age Day 21   Moon Sign Virgo*

This is a high point in the month, during which you are turning your attention towards plans you have been wishing to put into action for some time. Your general level of energy is high and good luck attends many of your efforts. Act now for maximum benefit in the days and weeks to come.

21 WEDNESDAY ☿ *Moon Age Day 22   Moon Sign Virgo*

Your personal magnetism is beginning to show and with Christmas only a few of days away you are able to create a positively magical setting, particularly for younger people. Rewards come along as a result of decisions and actions you took in the past, maybe bringing better financial wherewithal.

22 THURSDAY ☿ *Moon Age Day 23   Moon Sign Libra*

Don't get into pointless arguments that prove nothing today. Stay away from discussions, unless you know you will react positively and be prepared to spend an hour or two on your own if you are aware that your grumpy side is showing. By the evening, you should be back on form.

23 FRIDAY ☿ *Moon Age Day 24   Moon Sign Libra*

Love affairs are well highlighted today, as is travel, maybe to see people you haven't shared an hour or two with for quite a long time. Although you might be bullied into doing things that go against the grain, you could be quite surprised in the end. It is worth putting yourself out.

24 SATURDAY ☿ *Moon Age Day 25   Moon Sign Scorpio*

Last minute arrangements might well be keeping you on the hop but the sort of activities in which you are involved supply their own momentum. You won't believe everything you hear at present and will be determined to follow your own advice, especially in situations that involve finance.

25 SUNDAY ☿ *Moon Age Day 26   Moon Sign Scorpio*

Look out for an extremely interesting and varied sort of Christmas Day. It could be that not everyone in your family and friendship circle is having quite as good a time as you are and this could lead to extra effort on your part. The most enjoyable associations today come via close, personal attachments.

26 MONDAY ☿ *Moon Age Day 27   Moon Sign Scorpio*

Your social instincts are very definitely engaged today and you can be the best company imaginable. This is fortunate as, being Boxing Day, today is far from being a normal sort of Monday. There are gains to be made through love and new friendship so enjoy all that the holiday has to offer.

27 TUESDAY ☿ *Moon Age Day 28   Moon Sign Sagittarius*

It is the home-based side of Christmas that appeals to you the most around this time, though you are chatty, carefree and very good company in any situation. There could be presents of a very singular nature still to come your way, and one or two of them may come from a most unexpected direction.

28 WEDNESDAY ☿ *Moon Age Day 29   Moon Sign Sagittarius*

If you feel slightly dispirited in certain respects, you can take heart from the knowledge that things will look better, and busier, as the day goes on. You become more socially inclined and could be feeling the need to travel around more. There are still moments during the day when you would best enjoy curling up with a good book.

29 THURSDAY ☿ *Moon Age Day 0   Moon Sign Capricorn*

The time is right to establish good relations with just about anyone, even people who have not been your favourites in the past. There is a good chance that you are being taken more seriously now and that you might attract, as a friend, someone who was never very kind to you in years gone by.

30 FRIDAY ☿ *Moon Age Day 1 Moon Sign Capricorn*

Communication issues are to the fore today and you need to make sure that you get any message across intact. Don't be too quick to judge others for merely doing the same things that you yourself have done in the past. It would be sensible to take a sympathetic point of view wherever possible today.

31 SATURDAY ☿ *Moon Age Day 2 Moon Sign Capricorn*

Encounters with others may inspire some new ideas today. Get out and about as much as possible and certainly aim to have a really good time tonight. As for New Year resolutions, it might be best to leave them on the shelf for the moment. You will think more clearly about them once January actually arrives.

RISING SIGNS FOR VIRGO

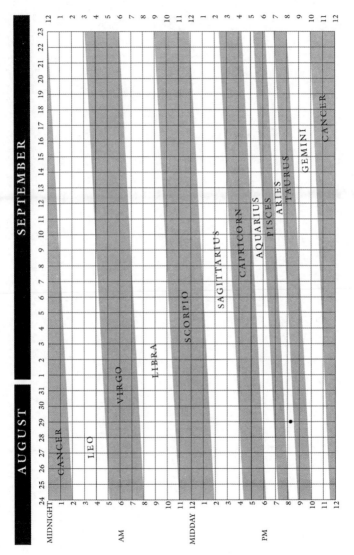